76-43

792.073
K869r   Krawitz, Herman E
           Royal American Symphonic Theater; a radical proposal for a
        subsidized professional theater ₍by₎ Herman E. Krawitz with
        Howard K. Klein.   New York, Macmillan ₍1975₎

           xi, 211 p.   21 cm.

           Bibliography: p. 204-205.

           1. Theater   United States.   I. Klein, Howard Kenneth, 1931-   joint
        author.   II. Title.

        PN2266.K7   792'.0973   73-21296
        ISBN 0-02-566700-9   MARC
                                                            895
        Library of Congress   74

Royal American Symphonic Theater

Royal American Symphonic Theater

*A Radical Proposal for a
Subsidized Professional Theater*

Herman E. Krawitz
with Howard K. Klein

Macmillan Publishing Co., Inc.
NEW YORK

Collier Macmillan Publishers
LONDON

This book is respectfully dedicated to The American Actor and Actress—to those who aspire and those who achieve—who have brought or will bring color, drama, life and truth to our stages; and to the nobility inherent in the theater profession.

Macmillan Publishing Co., Inc.
866 Third Avenue, New York, N. Y. 10022
Collier Macmillan Canada, Ltd.

Library of Congress Cataloging in Publication Data
Krawitz, Herman E
  Royal American Symphonic Theater.
  Includes bibliographical references.
   1. Theater—United States. I. Klein, Howard
Kenneth, 1931- joint author. II. Title.
PN2266.K7   792'.0973   73-21296
ISBN 0-02-566700-9

First Printing 1975

Printed in the United States of America

Contents

Preface and
Acknowledgments

THE IDEA FOR THIS book began with a casual conversation I had with Richard Oldenburg in 1964. In the years since it grew until the present collaboration was formed, and the end product resulted. Here is the background for that conversation and a description of some of the problems in American theater then. Curiously, in ten years the picture has not changed much.

In December of 1964 I was serving on a jury, the foreman of which was Richard Oldenburg. He was then managing editor of Macmillan; later he became director of the Museum of Modern Art. There was much time for talk, as there always is in jury rooms, and we found ourselves discussing the turbulent times of the Lincoln Center Repertory Theater, whose problems were daily front-page stories in *The New York Times*. Elia Kazan and Robert Whitehead, two seasoned theater professionals, had resigned as co-directors of the new Repertory Theater at Lincoln Center, in part because I had been approached by Lincoln Center officials to take over the job. I was then an assistant general manager of the Metropolitan Opera with a long involvement in theater. The controversy raged for a week or so on the *Times'* front pages, then was retired to the back pages for another week. I had declined the invitation to succeed Kazan and Whitehead. Oldenburg and I discussed the problems of the Lincoln Center Theater, of American theater in general and what, if any, were the potential solutions.

My involvement in theater began in my sophomore year at City College in Manhattan, at which time—on July 1, 1947, to be exact—I opened my first theater, the University Playhouse at Mashpee, Massachusetts. It was a summer theater, and for six years after that I worked in four theaters as manager and producer, organizing and supervising the construction or renovation of the theater at Mashpee, the Falmouth Playhouse, the Cape Cod Melody Tent and the South Shore Music Circus. It was great fun and I learned the basics of theater production and management. In 1953 the Metropolitan Opera hired me as a consultant on labor matters and then asked me to stay to take charge of productions. I did, and soon found my duties growing to include managing business affairs, being secretary to the board of directors and, finally, becoming assistant general manager under Sir Rudolf Bing.

In those early years with the Met I also found time to do outside consulting on theater work for such far-flung organizations as the Music Carnival in Cleveland, the Cherry County Playhouse in Traverse City, Michigan, and the Valley Forge and Westbury music fairs. In 1955 the Met began looking into the possibilities of constructing a new home for itself and I was asked to help plan for the new house at Lincoln Center. In this capacity I represented the company and the board in all liaison work with Wallace K. Harrison, the architect. In order to do this I made a personal on-site study of many American and European theaters and opera houses.

During that jury-room conversation with Oldenburg, who knew some of my history and who was as disturbed as most professionals about the Kazan-Whitehead resignation and the severe problems that seemed endemic to the new Lincoln Center Theater, he suggested that someone should write a book laying out the ground rules for theater management in such a way that future theater planners might avoid the kinds of pitfalls that were robbing the Lincoln Center Repertory Theater of its promise. And, he said, "Herman, why don't you write it?"

I had little time, however, and although the project was enticing, put it aside. In 1966 Dean Robert Brustein of the Yale Drama School asked me to organize and head a Department of Theater Administration. In order to do this I began to collect mounds of information—clippings, books, personal diaries—related to theater management and the problems of art and business. The course material also began to feed the idea of the book.

In 1971 I asked Howard Klein, a former *New York Times* music critic, to collaborate. He was then associate director for arts and humanities at The Rockefeller Foundation, and he shared my concern for the future of theater in America.

I left the Metropolitan Opera on July 1, 1972, exactly twenty-five years from the date of the opening of the old Mashpee Playhouse—and was subsequently asked to serve as the director of the newly created Leonard Davis Center of the Performing Arts at City College, my old alma mater, where it had all begun. I continue to be active independently as a planner and producer and consultant in performing arts projects.

Mr. Klein's experiences in theater, aside from acting with the City Island Summer Stock company in 1957, have been largely vicarious. But during his years with The Rockefeller Foundation since 1967 he has worked with leaders in theater from all over the world and has come to the conclusion that the root problems in American theater are not soluble by anything less than the most comprehensive approach. Millions of dollars have been poured into commercial and noncommercial American theater and yet the profession itself remains one of the lowest paid in our economy, one in which its practitioners rely on Unemployment Insurance. But that is a major point of the book, so more on it later.

As there is nothing new under the sun, much of what is said in this book is not new. Although my concepts and many of my solutions were arrived at independently, I discovered, in the course of preparing the manuscript, an important book on the theory of theater management that parallels my own thinking. The book is *Scheme and Estimates for a National Theater*, the collaborative effort of William Archer and Harley Granville-Barker, published in England in 1904 and in America in 1908. These turn-of-the-century authors called for the institutionalization of theater in England, arguing against those who were lobbying for a national opera that England's great strength in the arts was not music or dance, but rather, the theater. It was a prophetic book, but the unwillingness of the English to support institutionalized theater resulted in a delay of forty-five years before Parliament empowered the treasury to make funds available for what was to be the National Theatre. This was done in 1949, but another twenty years had to pass before the money actually materialized. The National Theatre passes the test of a major theater institution: it presents variety, maintains a tradition, yet is proudly innovative. It trades fairly heavily on the classics, old and new, but has never, from the beginning, been either parochial or chauvinistic. It has consistently recognized a duty—if not a primary one—to modern playwrights. Its artistic director, Sir Laurence Olivier, once defended the National Theatre's comprehensive programming policy with the statement: "The National Theatre can never be what the public wants if it isn't allowed sometimes to be what the public doesn't want."

This book is a call to action in the 1970s for the creation of a great theater institution in America—a Royal American Symphonic Theater, or several such theaters —to provide Americans with the best of what the venerable art of theater can offer in a modern American context. I do not accept the attempts made thus far in this country to institutionalize theater, nor am I willing to abide by the old notion that Broadway is what American theater should be. Further, I am convinced that there is an appetite in our country for theater art, and that if Americans were given a taste of the best of theater, they would come back for more—and they would support it.

We wish to thank all those who have helped us with this book, especially: Naomi and Bruce Bliven, Jr.; Sydelle Lichtman; Rose Connelly, Walt Jones, Thomas Kerrigan, Cynthia Parker and many other Yale students; Rhoda Krawitz and Patricia Windrow Klein and our children, who patiently withstood the trials of book writing; James Neyland and William Griffin, our editors; many theater professionals and others who advised and helped us to broaden our understanding of the art and business of theater; The Rockefeller Foundation for the period of residency in 1973 at its International Conference Center at Bellagio, Italy, which enabled Mr. Klein to make major revisions in the text; and, of course, Richard Oldenburg.

Royal American
Symphonic Theater

1

The Future of Theater
Has Arrived:
What Went Wrong?

SINCE THE TURN OF the twentieth century a dream of American theater has existed in the minds of professionals, an elusive dream which many have struggled to bring into being. It is of a theater broad in scope and purpose, a theater of balance in which entertainment mingles with enlightenment, mirth with majesty, and in which artistic awareness includes social consciousness. Great artists have tried to create this theater with varying, always temporary, success. Where, today, are our Great Theater Companies? Reading American theater history books is like walking through a cemetery, the noble gravestones to right and left: The New Theater, the Theater Guild, the Civic Repertory Theater, The Group Theater, The Mercury Theater, The Federal Theater, and on and on. The latest stone to be put into place reads: The Lincoln Center Repertory Theater, R.I.P. Of all theater failures, perhaps this was the bitterest disappointment.

Born into the family of internationally important Lincoln Center constituents—the Metropolitan Opera, the New York Philharmonic, the New York City Center Opera and Ballet, the Juilliard School—the Repertory Theater saw ten years of some mild triumphs and much that was commonplace before its demise in 1973. Its last season in

1972–1973 was, ironically, its best. But it died and was replaced in the autumn of 1973 by the New York Shakespeare Festival Theater of Joseph Papp. Thus ended a sad chapter of American theater history. The Lincoln Center Repertory Theater's struggle with directors, boards, audiences and playwrights is a capsulized version of how American theater has fared in this century.

A nonprofit theater, it came into being against a background of American theater dominated by Broadway. Since most Americans hearing the word "theater" think "Broadway," an analysis of Broadway is important. Theater is the one performing art that has the possibility of making a profit, of flourishing as a commercial enterprise. Profit-making is the motive force behind Broadway. If $10 million is invested in one year in Broadway shows, new plays and musicals, at least 75 percent of that investment fails to produce income—but the remaining 25 percent frequently earns more than the $10 million. The central artistic focus of Broadway is the new play. A play that is new can be owned and therefore exploited to maximize profits. Stars are a part of Broadway's life, but stars tend to be made by new plays (although the reverse can happen too). In a system where the play is seen as a potential money-making property, the property's the thing. Therefore a playwright's theater is predominantly a commercial theater, a theater to make money, to amuse, titillate, divert. Broadway is for entertainment, and the grim mask of the comic-tragic insignia is rarely worn because tragedy is simply less entertaining than comedy. Being less appealing, it is by nature less marketable, so serious plays tend to be slighted. Broadway is an unbalanced, inartistic theater by definition, although its technical qualities and some performers may be of the highest caliber.

The rise of nonprofit theater in America has been reflected in the gradual invasion of Broadway by non-commercial producers. This change in style is now being accepted as an irreversible tide. Some predict that commercial producing will be a minority activity by 1980. Signaling this is the Pulitzer Prize in drama, awarded in 1969, 1970 and 1973 to plays developed by nonprofit theaters. (Howard Sackler's *The Great White Hope*, the 1969 winner, was first done by the Arena Stage of Washington, D.C., while Charles Gordone's *No Place To Be Somebody* and Jason Miller's *That Championship Season*, which won in 1970 and 1973 respectively, were developed by the New York Shakespeare Festival.)

Broadway's highest award, the Antoinette Perry (or "Tony"), is presented by the League of New York Theatres and Producers. From 1969 to 1974, four of its six awards for best plays were given to nonprofit theaters. In 1974 the competition for prizes was dominated by non-commercial organizations. Three of the four best-play nominees and one of the three musicals were nonprofit; and 31 of the 67 individuals nominated for acting, design, direction or choreography were nominated for work done at nonprofit houses. The impact nonprofit theater is having on a traditionally commercial enterprise is evident not only in numbers but in quality of production, seriousness of content, relevance to contemporary life.

As Broadway's "fabulous invalid" acquires new life, it is important to recognize that although the form of operation may be changing—David Merrick giving way to Joseph Papp—the framework remains! The ultimate value lies in the play and its author, not in the performer and his company.

In 1956 President Dwight D. Eisenhower shoved a silver spade into the gritty earth of a cleared lot on Broadway at Sixty-fourth Street and broke ground for what may have been the greatest single shot in the arm American high culture has ever received. The grand marble acropolis of Lincoln Center that was to rise on this site was to be home for opera, symphony, dance and *theater*. Since no extant theater was deemed acceptable for inclusion, one was created. Delight and disbelief gripped the theater community, which had witnessed one attempt after another to create noncommercial theaters in New York. The belief was that a great decade of theater would dawn with the rising of the Repertory Theater of Lincoln Center. It would have a permanent company of great actors to do the finest plays of the past and present. To reread a *New York Times* article by Maurice Zolotow heralding this golden age now, after the death of the Repertory Theater, is to be reminded of the hopes and aspirations that have quickened the pulse of theater professionals through the century.

"Sometime in January, 1961," the article begins tremulously, "Elia Kazan and Robert Whitehead will take leave of the commercial theater. This is the first seismic tremor in what may prove to be a great earthquake in the American theater, comparable to the effect of the Theater Guild during the nineteen twenties and of the Group Theater during the nineteen thirties. For these two men have been appointed as the guiding spirits of the Repertory Theater Association, which will be a part of the Lincoln Center for the Performing Arts, now going up on fourteen acres of ground uptown. The repertory company will inhabit a new theater—the first to be built in New York since the Ethel Barrymore in 1928. . . . Our leading playwrights—including Tennessee Williams and Arthur Miller, who have expressed enthusiasm for the new theater—will be giving their plays to this ensemble. . . . Then, thirty of our leading actors, including Geraldine Page and Christopher Plummer, will be removed for a long time from the pool of talent available to the bourgeois impresarios of the Forty-fourth Street ambience." Long rehearsal periods, up to eight months, would make possible the superb ensemble playing long admired in European companies, but the greatest shock to the established theater would be the sweep and scope of the productions themselves. Elia Kazan excitedly described "a theater of color and spectacle, of mobility on the use of stage dynamics, a utilization of the arts of the painter, the singer, the choreographer, the pantomimist."

The Repertory Theater would be so successful it might offer unfair competition to Broadway. "Will this repertory theater," Zolotow asked, "being subsidized, prove an unfairly competitive threat to the David Merricks and the Kermit Bloomgardens?" According to Kazan and White-head, no; rather the theater would be "an energizing force for the commercial theater because it may develop new writers, new acting talents, and new techniques of rehearsal and staging that can be integrated into the established theater." Excitement was so keen that some 44,000 people wanted subscriptions even before the company was created!

One can only sympathize with those who shared the high optimism of 1961. The reality of the theater was something less than brilliant. Founded on sound concepts, it was to be a nonprofit theater whose annual projected deficit was to be met through donations. The first board of the Lincoln Center Rep was headed by Robert Hoguet and it saw the new company through its first stage of life with some promise. That was the planning stage. But when it came to actual producing and meeting real deficits, the foundation of the theater trembled and never settled. Kazan and Whitehead, two theatrical professionals with considerable expertise and background, began putting together a company in 1962 for the theater, which was to be completed in 1965. The company first performed on an apron stage in Washington Square and earned mixed but on the whole encouraging reviews. The board, however, worried, and this group, which included people distinguished in their own fields but not in theater,

pulled a coup in 1964 which stripped Kazan and Whitehead of their leadership and brought in as replacements
two regionally important but nationally unknown professionals, Herbert Blau and Jules Irving. The board hoped
this pair would rescue the theater from what it saw as
impending disaster. Not impending *artistic* disaster, but
a deficit the board deemed too large to raise. The board's
unwillingness to assume responsibility for the mandated
deficits was the root weakness of the theater, although
the artistic work was often blamed for its troubles.

Herbert Blau left the theater in 1966 and Jules Irving
continued to run it until the end. It is only fair to give Mr.
Irving credit for doing as well as he did under the circumstances. There was constant trouble from the board
about deficits, and at one point the board was ready to
sell out its second theater, the Forum, to the City Center,
which wanted to make of it a cinematheque and film
library. Walter Kerr, drama critic for *The New York
Times*, saw this as another example of the legitimate theater's inevitable giving way to film.

What went wrong between the excited announcement
of the new Lincoln Center theater and its failure of realization? Was it that America was not ready for the emer-
gence of a great theater? Or that those who were
entrusted with bringing this theater to life failed to
understand the nature of the art form of theater and its
confusing relationship to the commercial enterprise system of Broadway? Did they want art and money-making
hits too?

Time and again, the future of the theater has arrived,
not as forecast by artists, professionals and critics, but
as a disappointment. Another wistful period of expectation was enjoyed by professionals when the new
theater was announced for the John F. Kennedy Center.
While plans were still being made in 1967 Howard
Taubman wrote excitedly about the possibility of a

national theater, comparable to England's National Theatre. His article in *The New York Times* underscores how deeply felt is the need for an important American theater. "A national theater company," he wrote, "based at the Kennedy Center, could be a powerful force not only in Washington but in the nation. It would have to be a troupe of the highest calibre. Britain's National Theatre, which, under the leadership of Sir Laurence Olivier, started strong and has continued to be impressive, is the kind of enterprise to which the Kennedy Center should aspire." The Kennedy Center opened in 1971 and the new Eisenhower Theater building was a delight, but no company was there to fill it. We did not get the "powerful force not only in Washington but in the nation" of which Taubman wrote.

Theater is a guiding force in our society, as it has been in societies since the dawn of civilization. At its best theater can uplift the mind and sensibilities. At its worst it can debase them. Theater is no better than the society from which it grows and for which it is intended. Federico García Lorca, the great Spanish playwright, said,

> "The theater is one of the most expressive and useful instruments for building up a country; it is the barometer of its greatness or decline. An intelligent theater, well oriented in all its branches from tragedy to vaudeville, can change the sensibility of a people within a few years; a disintegrated theater, with clumsy hooves instead of wings, can cheapen and lull into sleep an entire nation. . . ."[1]

What kind of theater does America have? Two kinds: live theater, where live actors perform for live audiences; and canned theater, in which film or videotape replays

---

[1] Federico García Lorca, 1935, special performance of *Yerma*, Teatro Español, Madrid; speech addressed to actors and workers of the theater.

live performances. It is beyond the scope of this book to analyze film and television as theater, though they impinge directly on a full understanding of American theater. It can be said and readily accepted, however, that live theater has always influenced film and television by developing creative talents as well as dramatic concepts and properties for their use, and it continues to do so to some extent. Theater has been the potting shed for the mass media, which have transplanted its shoots into the consciousness of the whole world. Few earthlings have seen live American theater, but much of the world's population has become involved in the products of that theater.

Film and television both relate directly to our theater —more specifically, to Broadway. In the life cycle of our live and electronic drama, the Broadway play often is the progenitor. After a successful Broadway run, a play is sold to a film company, and from a hit film, a television series is produced. One example is Neil Simon's *The Odd Couple*, an amusing and trivial situation comedy that played as a hit on Broadway, was made into a film and then a television series. The impact of this one example can only be understood in the context of the importance of American films all over the world and the saturation of foreign television by American products.

Besides Broadway, sources for film and television include books and specially written or conceived materials. But the mentality governing the drama of film or television shares the commercial bias of Broadway. Amusement—even of a gory or sordid nature—prevails.

Assuming that nothing *is* that does not have a purpose (who was it who said that a weed was a plant man had not found a use for yet?), then what is, or could be, the purpose of live theater? Essentially it is an expression of man's individual and collective dreams and fantasies, anxieties and frustrations, triumphs and failures, through a medium in which people pretend they are what they are not so that a story can be told, a dramatic conflict set and resolved.

How do we use theater? American theater has a long history and in some ways a brilliant one. There have been great American actors and actresses, playwrights, theater artists of all description. Until the invention of film in the early years of the twentieth century theater was *the* popular diversion. Everyone went to the theater—to be instructed, uplifted, provoked, but primarily to be entertained. Entertainment has always been popular and people have always been willing to pay money to be diverted for a few hours from their own troubles. Theater was a business. A big business.

When the touring stock companies died off in the first decade of the 1900s, they were mourned, and a vigorous Little Theater movement sprang up. These theaters were noncommercial, amateur, the salt of the earth, but not very good in most cases. Professionalism was preserved in the cities, where the theaters continued to do well. The Shubert organization, a huge chain of theaters across the country, came into being, along with The Syndicate, and these two powerful businesses literally ran every kind of theater across America—classic drama, new plays, vaudeville. In the wild economic excesses of the 1920s theater grew out of proportion, with most of the activity taking place in New York City, which was the country's theater center and headquarters of the monopolistic touring organizations.

What happened on Broadway then was to shape the future of American theater for better or for worse, even though the heyday of Broadway only lasted for about ten years prior to the 1929 Wall Street crash and the introduction of the talking picture. Theater in the twenties became a speculator's paradise where a fortune could be made overnight by adroit exploitation of a new show fitted with the right star. In this milieu the craze was for the "hit play," with a small army of playwrights and composers grinding out what they hoped would be the new hit. Appealing to the mass market, this strictly commercial enterprise attracted some of the finest artists of the day. It was a theater to amuse, to divert. Little thought was given to art, but because of the quality of some of the artists attracted by the glint of gold on Broadway, enduring works were actually created—though not many.

It is interesting to go back and read contemporary accounts of this brazen, money-hungry period of American theater, and one book, published in 1929, was remarkably pointed in its criticisms and predictions. *Box Office* was authored by the journalist, John Anderson, who minced no words. He called the splurge of theater speculation in the 1920s "a debauch of irresponsible production." In 1928 more than sixty theaters were operating on Broadway, twenty-five of them doing a flourishing business on a regular basis and the others being used by speculators, and producers were frenetically seeking new hits. Anderson commented wryly on the scene: "The alleged American genius for business has had a permeating influence upon the American theater. It is widely looked upon as a business by the people who manipulate it and the people who patronize it." Now Anderson was not against the new play as a concept. English theater had thrived for centuries on its great writers, and the playwright was an important entity in England (at least posthumously). He was not against Broadway-as-playwright's-theater, but only against the commercialism that was the apparent sole arbiter of taste and quality. Theater, he said, is never greater than its dramatists. The greatest periods of English theater were those in which three elements—the artistic, the social, and the economic —were firmly and inescapably held together under royal patronage. When an art form is subjected to that most doubtful of human institutions—majority rule—artistic quality must dissipate. By making the box office king, the Broadway producers effectively reduced to near-zero the chances that art would emerge from the wings.[2]

All the while, however, there were true artists working the Street, many of them playing the game by Broadway's rules. Spurning the trend, the powerful Theater Guild supported the cause of art, seeking an international repertory of dramas that had intellectual mettle and artistic vision. Chartered in 1919, the Guild was an offshoot of an earlier venture, the Washington Square Players. The Guild's mentors were Theresa Helburn, Lawrence Langner, Phillip Moeller, Lee Simonson, Maurice Wertheim and Helen Westley. In one year it had plays running in six different Broadway houses; in another it had plays in four houses plus seven companies on tour. This activity revitalized the dying road which ultimately built the Guild's subscribers to 30,000 in the tour cities. The Guild provided a place of stability for young talents to mature away from commercial pressures. Among them were Alfred Lunt, Lynn Fontanne, Edward G. Robinson, Harold Clurman, Margalo Gilmore, George Abbott and Lee Strasberg.

If commercial Broadway was the Anti-Christ, the Guild was Mother Church. Brooks Atkinson called it "the most dynamic and the most creative organization on Broadway. . . . The Guild annihilated provinciality in the American theater. Once it was established, Broadway became an active part of the theater of the world."[3]

The Guild was the stronghold for idealists and artists of all callings. They were, in Atkinson's phrase, "Utopians

[2] John Anderson, *Box Office*, New York, Jonathan Cape and Harrison Smith, 1929, pp. 10, 11.
[3] Brooks Atkinson, *Broadway*, New York, Macmillan, 1971, p. 208.

... not interested in making money. They were interested in establishing an art theater with modern standards."[4] With its utopian ideals, the Guild stood in direct opposition to the mentality of Broadway's commercial producers. Its fight for art over commerce symbolized the struggle theater in America is still engaged in, for the conflict between speculative productions to make money and theater for art's sake continues today.

Though the Guild was the most comprehensive theater we have had, and its ideals and goals were always high, it was too specialized and too close to the very commercial system its founders hoped it would combat if not supplant. In 1921, the third season of the Theater Guild's life, Theresa Helburn, a co-founder, said it was an attempt to marry art and business. She thought they were incompatible because "any marriage between the two results in innumerable compromises." Although the Guild was not run for private profit but was an actor's cooperative offering minimum salaries and a percentage of profits to the actors, it was not deficit-funded and therefore had to rely primarily on box-office receipts. Perhaps the incredible vitality of Broadway (which produced several hundred shows a year in the 1920s) provided the right environment for the Guild and enabled it to prove its thesis that "there is a place for purer art than the commercial theater gives us or can give us." The Guild's board included theater and nontheater people, who chose the plays. Touring was extensive, with subscribers in major cities around the country. Plays, such as Andreyev's *He Who Gets Slapped*, were converted into films. The Guild related beautifully to its "community," the audience. In Helburn's words, "We generally approximate in miniature the taste of the public we exist for, not the public of the commercial theater, of claptrap farce, of melodrama, of comic

[4] *Ibid.*, p. 209.

opera, but the public that wants reality, sincerity, and beauty—the only public we are trying to reach."[5]

As the number of theaters on Broadway and the amount of production shriveled in the 1930s, that public was less and less able to support the Theater Guild. Had the approach been more comprehensive, perhaps the Guild could have realized its dream of continuity and a permanent company of actors. It might have become our great theater, but it is idle to speculate. One cannot have continuity and a flourishing of the arts based exclusively on earnings.

That the Guild failed to become our national theater was plain to contemporaries, even in its heyday. Edith J. R. Isaacs wrote in 1927 (the peak of activity of American theater, with Broadway riding a dizzying crest) that America had failed to develop a theater because this country began just when European theater had fallen to its lowest level. Her analysis called for leadership rather than economic protection, but she erred in this judgment. There were leaders, but no theater institutions capable of properly utilizing leadership. Isaacs came close to seeing the need for institutionalization, while not spelling it out. She probably could not see beyond the promise of Broadway and presumed that artistic theater could actually thrive there. She wrote, "When the American theater develops leaders big enough to coordinate its energies and talents, the theater will take form. Until then, all we see is the trend."[6]

The Guild's record of achievements represents the highest attainments of American theater. It had begun as a small experimental theater in the 1918–1919 season and hit its prime in the middle and late 1920s. The falling off of business in the 1930s and 1940s effected a

---

[5] Theresa Helburn, "Art and Business: A Record of the Theatre Guild, Inc.," *Theatre Arts Magazine*, Vol. V, 1921.

[6] Edith J. R. Isaacs, ed., *Theatre*, Books for Libraries, 1927.

gradual decline of activity until in its fiftieth season, 1968–1969, only one play was produced.

A major offshoot of this attempt to develop a successful formula for producing an artistically-oriented theater was The Group Theater. Its goals were noble, its ideals lofty. The Group's manifesto was a banner raised for Art. Heavily involved in left-wing ideology, influenced profoundly by Stanislavski and the Moscow Art Theater, the Group broke away from the Guild in an amicable way and immediately attracted attention. The Group would accomplish what the Guild had not. The manifesto said, in part, "A good play for us is not one which measures up to some literary standard of 'art' or 'beauty' but one which is the image or symbol of the living problems of our time."[7]

Harold Clurman, co-founder of the Group and former director with the Guild, wrote in 1931, "We believe that the individual can achieve his fullest stature through the identification of his own good with the good of his group, a group which he himself must help to create."[8] This defined the Group's artistic policy, which included a partiality for social realism. An attempt was made to keep actors on minimum salary for a six-year period so they could develop their skills and the ensemble qualities the directors sought. But the economic footing of the Group was precarious, for it, too, was rooted in the Broadway system, and it failed because it could not produce enough box-office hits to live.

The Group was the precursor of the guerrilla theaters of the 1960s. Brooks Atkinson called them "evangelists who had little capacity for fun, and that was their only weakness on the stage. In an art form that tries to give

[7] John Gassner, "The World and the Theater," *Theater Arts Monthly*, May 1932.

[8] Harold Clurman, "A Critique of American Theater," *Drama Magazine*, April 1931.

pleasure, they worked too hard and too rigidly."[9] But the Group produced important plays, developed the talents of playwright Clifford Odets and was responsible for developing such actors as Franchot Tone, Morris Carnovsky, John Garfield, Luther Adler, and the director Elia Kazan. A major legacy of the Group is the theoretical school of acting it espoused—The Actor's Studio. This application of the so-called Stanislavski method continued to dominate American acting, for better or worse, in theater, film and television throughout the 1960s.

One of the chief weaknesses of the Group's policies was its business practices, in which it followed traditional commercial habits of optioning a play and waiting in line at the Shubert office for a theater to be available. It condemned the commercial theater of Broadway but nevertheless played the theater game by Broadway's rules. In the words of one contemporary, "They, who of all people should have striven to achieve the flexible status of a permanent, low-priced People's theater, were condemned by their directors to play intermittently for the carriage trade" at Broadway prices and for the usual precarious runs.[10] Harold Clurman, aware of this, aptly stated, "The basic defect in our activity was that while we tried to maintain a true theatre policy artistically, we proceeded economically on a show-business basis. Our means and our ends were in fundamental contradiction. Our past— the past which brought forth what I strongly believe was the most important theatrical accomplishment of the thirties—has shown what could be done in the worst circumstances. This compromise (running the Group on an unsound basis) was forced on the Group for ten years. But it is a compromise I no longer desire to make."[11] After

[9] Atkinson, *Broadway*, p. 292.

[10] John Houseman, *Run-Through*, New York, Simon and Schuster, 1972, p. 411.

[11] Harold Clurman, *The Fervent Years*, New York, Hill & Wang Dramabook (paperback), 1957, p. 263.

a decade of struggle the Group's directors realized that an art theater could not exist on show biz principles, that box office would never support idealism. The Group was enormously influential, but it, too, lacked comprehensiveness.

How many times has that banner emblazoned "Art Theater" been raised only to fall again because of the inability of organizers to think in large enough terms—financially and artistically? Noble phrases didn't save the APA-Phoenix Repertory Company of T. Edward Hambleton and Ellis Rabb. In a letter to the editor in *The New York Times* Rabb said, "The time has come for the theater to recognize that it has a responsibility as a platform from which to answer as well as to question, to confirm as well as to doubt, to maintain as well as to experiment. . . . It is our belief that the theater must now vitally recall its greatest opportunity. It must invoke its heritage. It must reinvolve its greatest instrument—language. The plays we have chosen [to produce] are distinguished not only by the originality of *what* they have to say about the human condition, but also by *how* they say it."

This call seemed comprehensive, but the theater itself only produced from four to six plays a year and therefore did not present much of a spectrum. In 1971 another call to bring a national theater into being was heard, this time from Joseph Papp. His call was based on a scheme that would involve the federal government in a program of financing tours of regional theater productions to other cities in order to reach wider audiences with the best plays and productions of existing American nonprofit theater. The Shakespeare Festival represented in the early 1970s the most influential American theater, producing adaptations of Shakespeare, such as the rock-musical version of *Two Gentlemen of Verona* (which was produced for free admission in Central Park in 1971 and successfully transferred to a Broadway house in the fall of that year for a long, happy run—at Broadway prices), and developing new plays, such as David Rabe's *Sticks and Bones* (which was run for a limited time on Broadway—at a loss to the theater—and subsequently made into a television play, which was broadcast in the summer of 1973 over CBS).

Papp's company was the largest single employer of actors in America. But the Shakespeare Festival's policy was Broadway's—actors are hired or fired according to need. I am convinced that this policy has not and will not bring about any changes for the better in the profession.

How many other noble attempts have there been in New York to found the Great Art Theater? A short list would include, besides those already mentioned, The New Theater, a magnificent failure of millionaires to create an uptown theater which lasted from 1909 to 1911; the Civic Repertory Company of Eva Le Gallienne, 1926–1932, a notable venture in the direction of standard repertory in which the brilliant actress Nazimova performed with Le Gallienne; the huge WPA-financed Federal Theater, which employed more theater artists in more American theaters across the country than had ever worked before, and may have provided the only true heyday of American theater between 1936 and 1939, when it was scuttled by a Congress that was worried about Communists in the theater; the brilliant Mercury Theater, an outgrowth of the Federal, organized and run by Orson Welles and John Houseman, which ran for two glorious seasons from 1936 to 1938; the Playwrights' Company, 1938–1952, a joint effort of three major playwrights in rebellion against Broadway. And then there have been the City Center Drama Company of the middle 1940s, ANTA, The American Repertory Theater, Theater Incorporated, the original Phoenix and the Association of Producing Artists (parents of the now defunct APA–Phoenix) and the Lincoln Center Repertory Theater.

All these theaters shared some common ideals and goals. Most of them attracted important playwrights and actors and sought to provide protection for their art against the vagaries of a commercial system based upon the hit play. But not one theater was truly able to realize its dreams, largely because none was able to erect its theater on a financial base that would support its artistic goals. The dream they built on is summed up by a comment made by Daniel Frohman in 1911. He was then mourning the recent death of the stock companies, which had given American theater its strong backbone. He was interested in new plays, but saw the necessity of institutionalization for their proper artistic development. He wrote, "So the stock company, as it was known, is apparently a thing of the past; and yet I have still a lurking hope that a permanent company of actors for the production of new plays may yet be possible."[12] This dream has not been fulfilled.

A society gets the theater it deserves, and America got a divided theater, an antagonistic theater in which an artistic minority waged war against a money-minded majority. For those concerned with the art of theater, the weight of judgment tends to rest on the written play. But, as pointed out by John Anderson, the great playwright needs a balance of artistic, social and economic elements in which to function. And the economic side of the artistically aspiring theater has always been its debilitating weakness.

Not until the recent years of foundation support for the arts and of their increasing subsidization by state, federal and corporate entities has economic security for noncommercial theater been possible. But there is still a preventive factor in the attitudes of most Americans toward theater, an attitude shaped largely by the victo-

[12] Daniel Frohman, *Memories of a Manager*, New York, Doubleday, Page and Company, 1911.

rious wing of American theater—Broadway. Most Americans are convinced that "theater makes money." Why, every school child knows that to raise money to buy some cherished thing, all you have to do is put on a play and charge admission. We are all seduced by the show biz consciousness to some extent, especially when we buy tickets and sit in a large auditorium with more than a thousand seats. It is true that theater is so structured that if a show is a hit, money can be made on it. A lot of money, especially if the rights are sold to the movies or television. But we should not confuse theater-to-entertain, or to amuse, with (for want of a better word) artistic theater, in which the uppermost goal is not to make money but art, in which it is desired not merely to entertain but also to involve the playgoer in an important event. Our artistic theaters are attempts at Lorca's "sensitive and well-oriented theater." They are the civilizing forces of intellectual and social discussion, ferment, even rebellion, which help inform and change old attitudes. This theater can include new plays or new ways of looking at classics—even museum pieces and failures.

The new patterns of support for nonprofit theater have produced so-called regional theaters which aim at professionalism and high artistic quality. These have added something to our general culture, although few have equaled their own aspirations and certainly none has exerted sufficient force to offset the dominance of Broadway in the total theater life of the country. This can best be confirmed by examining their board structures and the kinds of deficits they are allowed to incur, the size of their organizations, the length of their seasons, the number of theaters each organization operates and, most importantly, the proportion of acting staff on long-term contract at livable wages. One quickly realizes that although our nonprofit theaters are trying to preserve and develop the art of theater in their cities, they are being confined to economies which permit barely a holding operation.

In my fervor for a professional performers' company, concentration on failings in theater history may seem to exclude recognition of the many virtues that have prevailed. Thus while I decry the nature of the industry on Broadway, there is no more staunch an advocate of the professional standards that have been achieved on the "street." Similarly, while I question the financial structure and therefore, the projected potential of rapidly proliferating small theater groups around the country, I am genuinely respectful of their daring and vigor.

What would be the ideal state of professional, edifying theater in America? As a standard of comparison, look to the music profession. It is a limited one into which each year thousands of students pour, their university or conservatory diplomas in hand. Though employment is limited, professionals are working in broad areas of entertainment, education and community service. The most painful disparities between the music and theater professions, however, are not on the mass level, although music does in fact offer more jobs than theater, but at the highest level, the level of artistic quality that young musicians aim for from the beginning of their training.

America boasts twenty-eight fine orchestras for symphonic music, a handful of which equal the best in the world. It is here that the music profession differs so drastically from theater and points the way to the survival and further development of theater art. To be sure, the orchestras have their financial difficulties. But they are happily solved year after year, with the result that our major cities can each claim an orchestra to be proud of. These orchestras employ from eighty to more than a hundred players each, several on fifty-two–week contracts at livable salaries. In addition to the twenty-eight are hundreds of other orchestras operating on a semiprofessional basis with short seasons and lower wages, but offering to classically trained musicians artistic outlets for their skills and providing access to symphonic music for wide segments of the public.

Why is the symphonic picture as fine as it is? (Any symphony manager would tell you it should be better!) Because from the beginning of the building of the orchestras in the last century it was hardly ever assumed that orchestras would make money. The royal tradition of support had inculcated the notion that ticket prices had to be subsidized to some extent, and wealthy Americans were always willing to patronize the cause of music. Thus, without money-making as a primary concern, symphonic institutions have had an orderly growth with salubrious results. Commercial music was allowed to go its own way, earning millions for its practitioners, while classical musicians stuck to their three B's. To compare the music and theater professions more specifically, list the major orchestras geographically: The Boston Symphony, The New York Philharmonic, The Philadelphia Orchestra, the Cleveland Orchestra, The Chicago Symphony and the Los Angeles Philharmonic. Is there a theater in those cities which is on an equal basis (1) artistically, in terms of world prestige, or (2) organizationally, in terms of full-time employment of a permanent ensemble of actors? No. Now list the next group of fine orchestras in their cities, zigzagging from West to East: San Francisco, Seattle, Salt Lake City, Denver, Minneapolis, St. Louis, Dallas, Houston, Detroit, Cincinnati, Louisville, New Orleans, Miami, Atlanta, Washington, D.C., Baltimore, and Buffalo. What theaters in those cities equal the orchestras? There is not one. No, not the Guthrie in Minneapolis, a quality theater, but incapable of mounting a season comparable to the Minneapolis Orchestra's, or on the same artistic level. Not the American Conservatory Theater in San Francisco, which is bigger than most and does admirable work, but again, lacks exceptional quality. The New York Shakespeare Festival Theater of New York does not pretend to try to keep together a company of virtuosos in acting who could match skills with the New York Philharmonic. Boston has no professional theater. Other cities have made valiant attempts at professional theater, but everywhere the story is the same.

The fault is not necessarily the theater's. We should be thankful for the ones we have, given the mentality of Americans regarding artistic theaters which says they should "make money." Their organizers deserve medals, all. But more important, they and their cities deserve access to truly high-level theater. If a World's Fair of Art were being planned and America could send only one orchestra, dance company and theater, it would be interesting to see the quality disparity between the first two categories and the theater company. The orchestra, mighty, confident, capable of playing anything from the most intimate music to the greatest orchestral canvases, would be exultant in competition. America would have a premier representative. Among dance company possibilities there would be the big ballets—the New York City Ballet, the American Ballet Theater, the Robert Joffrey Ballet—and the smaller but highly regarded companies of Martha Graham, Eliot Feld, Alvin Ailey and Alwin Nikolais, as well as companies in Utah, Pittsburgh, Washington and elsewhere. But among the theaters?

Theater in America lacks the kind of institutional protection that has enabled our musicians and dancers to practice their art with a distinction that has won world praise. The American theater desperately needs such excellence but has yet to attain it. Which of our theaters can mount a memorable cycle of Shakespeare, Molière, Shaw, O'Neill? None. Which theater can regularly attract the greatest artists in the profession to bring life to its stages in old and new dramas, from the Greeks to the newest experimentalists? None. We have had only fitful attempts. In music, however, a regal procession of brilliant players and singers works with our orchestras and opera companies, giving recitals over the land, and soloists earn their high fees by delivering the kind of artistry of which a country can be proud.

The purpose of this book is twofold: (1) to call attention to the condition of theater in America and the plight of our theater art in an environment that has devastated the theater profession, and (2) to suggest ways of improving that situation. It is hoped that theater professionals and others interested in theater will not only see the problems inherent in any plan that outlines "paper seasons" and projections of possible structures and funding, but will also help find the solutions, and above all will take new heart. So many artists have worked in the American theater and brought to it great distinction. That they have not stayed in the field because they were unable to find work, or were unable to accommodate their own standards to those of a beleaguered profession, is the point at issue.

It is time to proclaim that theater is important to American civilization, that we need our theaters of entertainment but we also need theaters of maturity, wisdom and enlightenment, theaters where artists may struggle together not just to eat, but to revivify our lives by their acting, designing, directing and playwrighting. We should not save the American theater for "educational purposes," nor to preserve a "cultural heritage," nor to prove that we are no longer colonials but a cultivated people. We should save the theater to please ourselves. And we should start by reforming the state of the profession and focusing our attention not so much on the economic welfare of the playwright (who may indeed be the voice of the theater of our time) but on the men and women who make theater possible—the actors. For the theater profession cannot rise higher than its actors. It is by emphasizing the performer that the music profession has reached high artistic levels and it will by lifting the actor to the status of a true professional that theater in America may come into its long-awaited prime.

2

The One-Way
Street of Theater

GREAT PLAYS EXIST BECAUSE of playwrights; playwrights
exist because of actors. Without groups of players for
writers to create for and with, what theater would there
be? From the Greeks on, Western dramatic literature has
rested on companies of actors. The actor is the medium
of expression of theater, the human vehicle by which
ideas and images set in dramatic conflict and resolution
are realized.

Acting has been called the most appreciated and least
understood of all the arts. To be an actor is to be blessed
with a rare sensitivity to human psychology and the ability to mimic, or, in the best actors, project authentic
emotions out of synthetic situations which, in Tolstoi's
words, have the quality of being able to infect the viewer
with those very emotions. The actor is the electricity in
the bulb of theater. Philip Weisman calls the actor (who
is mindful of inner truth) a contributor to psychological
insight.[1] Harold Clurman wrote, "The actor is (hopefully)
a creator. Samuel Johnson said that the actor only *recites*:
but no living playwright is happy if his actors do no more
than that. As a creator the actor has an artistic weight of

[1] Philip Weisman, *Creativity in Theater: a Psychoanalytic Study*,
Delta, 1965, p. 248.

25

his own—not to speak of other kinds of influence he may unadvisedly exert."[2] And the great Stanislavski once said, "Have a group of talented actors and you will have a play and a theater."

Many are drawn to acting, few are chosen. The aspiring young actor may see himself playing Hamlet, but in our American theater system he may be lucky to act in a TV commercial. Despite the rather gloomy future for theater's newcomers, thousands of students each year leave their schools armed with high hopes for success. It is common practice for collegiate education in the arts to ignore supply and demand. Regardless of the professional conditions, actors, musicians and other artists graduate into overcrowded fields far too limited for the increasing numbers of newly entering aspirants. If not told in school, the young actor soon learns that the acting profession operates within a cruel system of hurry-up-and-wait, which often functions like a one-way street right out of theater itself. The system includes some training, looking for work, trying to survive in a no-work profession by getting nontheater jobs and eventually being lured out of legitimate theater, which was often the primary goal, into films and television, which pay far better but are frequently artistically frustrating for the actor.

There have been complaints in recent years that American actors are ill-prepared for professional work. There is truth in this, for far too few educational institutions provide adequate preprofessional theater study. Howard Taubman, a *New York Times* critic looking at the picture of dramatic training in 1965, saw a higher level of instruction over the 1950s, but still felt that American acting had not yet become a "rationalized, cultivated craft" and that our acting standards had not advanced

2 Harold Clurman, *On Directing*, New York, Macmillan, 1972, p. 10.

measurably. Americans could do a few things well, such
as boisterous farce and realistic "slices of life," and there
was a "cheerful resilience for fast-moving, earthy comedy
of contemporary vintage." American actors could "glow in
musical comedy," but the range of the majority was limited. Taubman set the goal of theatrical training, as do I,
at nothing less than training for the classic stage. With
command in such a demanding milieu, the actor could
then "easily adapt himself to the demands of modern
drama, for he has all the basic equipment."[3]

Theater training in general is still mediocre. There are
a few bright spots, however, among them the comprehensive training programs at Carnegie-Mellon University in
Pittsburgh, Yale University, The Goodman Theater of
Chicago, New York University and the Juilliard School's
Drama Division. But even assuming a young actor has had
access to the best preprofessional training and experiences, where can he go?

He goes to where the jobs are. New York long ago cor-
nered the market for legitimate theater on Broadway,
Off Broadway and the experimental houses and lofts of
Off-Off Broadway. Actors who want stage experience
come to New York. It is also a center for television commercial manufacture and advertisement, though it
shares this distinction with Los Angeles, which claims the
second highest concentration of actors per population.
Actors in Los Angeles have little access to the legitimate
stage—there are only a handful of theaters there—so
most are looking for work in films, on television drama
series or in commercials. There are far more actors than
jobs in both places. For the neophyte, the chances of finding work in New York or Hollywood are dismally remote.
Actors are notoriously tenacious and may strive for years
before settling into another line of work. During their

[3] Howard Taubman, *The Making of the American Theater*, New
York, Coward-McCann, 1965, pp. 345–347.

period of struggle they frequently learn, not the skills they need to perfect their art, but the sad facts of life. Like Collodi's Pinocchio, who was promised fame and fortune as a star but who ended up in a bird cage, the American actor learns that the actor's life is less than full.

He learns, for example, that to be an actor in the legitimate theater is to be among the lowest paid of all workers, and that the amount of time spent on the job each year may be less than a factory worker's vacation. In 1957–1958 the 7,000 members of Actors Equity earned an average yearly income of only $2,000. In 1965 a study indicated that during an average week of a season only one-fifth of the active membership of Actors Equity was employed in the profession. In their landmark study, *Performing Arts: The Economic Dilemma*, Princeton economists William Bowen and William J. Baumol reported the following: "According to the 1960 census, 4.6 percent of musicians, 7.6 percent of male dancers, and 26.1 percent of actors were officially *unemployed* during the census week: they had no paid employment of any kind, *in or out of their chosen field*, and were seeking work. Among all males in the professional occupations, the unemployment rate was only 1.4 percent."[4]

If actors don't work, how do they live? An insight is given in this anecdote about the hurly-burly of Off-Off Broadway and actors' scramble for limited jobs. Off-Off Broadway's "diverse collection of noncommercial playhouses" is, according to Mel Gussow, writing in *The New York Times*, "the most productive theater in New York. It stages some 500 shows a year compared with 100 for Broadway and Off Broadway combined. Unlike its commercial cousins, Off-Off Broadway never stops. Plays open every week all year long. It is the process not the product

4 William G. Bowen and William J. Baumol, *Performing Arts: The Economic Dilemma*, New York, Twentieth Century Fund, 1966, pp. 127–128.

that is important. . . . The actors are in it for the love of it, and many of them have to support themselves elsewhere, making commercials, working as clerks, waitresses or cabdrivers, one reason why shows generally run only on weekends. Carla Joseph, one of the New York Theater Ensemble's playwrights, recalls that when she was casting her current play, '250 people showed up to read for 10 roles and one understudy.' "

Off-Off Broadway is New York's primal soup of theater. But are the actors really, as Gussow suggests, "in it for the love of it," meanwhile keeping body and soul together by waiting on tables, driving cabs, clerking? Is this why they spent four years at a university? Probably not. But what alternative is there at the bottom of the ladder, which is what Off-Off Broadway is, when the competition is so keen that 250 actors line up for eleven possible jobs? If this is a typical case, and if Off-Off Broadway mounts 500 shows a year, does that mean that for every show there may be another 250 actors lined up? If so, it would mean a pool of several thousand unemployed actors, assuming that some of the same actors tried out for many of the shows.

Perhaps it is proper for aspiring actors to apprentice in the Off-Off Broadway kitchen where work is scarce, pay low and hopes for the big break practically nil. The experimental, noncommercial, Off-Off Broadway scene is where actors prepare for the rigorous professionalism of Off Broadway, which, they hope, will lead to Broadway itself. Let us look at the next rung of the ladder, then, and see what hope of artistic or professional achievement is possible there.

The Off Broadway movement came into its own in 1952 with the Circle in the Square's Greenwich Village production of Tennessee Williams' *Summer and Smoke* with Geraldine Page. It was the first box-office hit below the theater district in thirty years, and spurred a gradual movement of producers south to seek smaller, cheaper theaters to serve as showcases for plays and talent. Within fifteen years Off Broadway became virtually indistinguishable from Broadway, the only distinction being that Broadway houses were larger, Broadway contracts more expensive. Because of the lower fees Off Broadway, more and more producers made money there. Some, in fact, made fortunes. Only handfuls of Off Broadway shows ever became hits, but actors and Actors Equity, which had long been lenient regarding the minimum wages for Off Broadway—wages so low they constituted an actors' subsidy of the theaters—realized that Off Broadway was no longer a showcase, a rung on the way up to Broadway, films and television, but had become an end in itself. There is a general misconception that Off Broadway and Off-Off Broadway embody a different idea from Broadway, and the claims to moral and artistic superiority are nonsensical.

The actors called a strike in November 1970, the reasons for which were obvious. Off Broadway ticket prices were frequently higher than those on Broadway! Pay scales were ludicrously low. The strike closed theaters, held up production and kept those actors fortunate enough to have jobs out of work, but a point was made. The spoils of this short stoppage were practically insignificant, however, although in percentage terms the gains seemed large. The actors won a 33⅓ percent raise from a minimum wage of $75 per week to $100 per week, which would be scaled up to $125 per week in the third year of the contract.

Clive Barnes, *The New York Times* drama critic, made some cogent observations on the strike. He wrote that the adapted theaters of Off Broadway were not large or attractive enough to equate with its new way of living. "There are almost as many risks involved in putting on an

Off Broadway show as there are in a Broadway show, and statistically the chances of a backer losing his shirt or an angel his halo are substantially greater Off Broadway than on." The economic pattern of Off Broadway theater demanded "that the theater be subsidized by the actors giving their services at something markedly lower than their true values."

If an actor survives the economic deprivation, not to speak of the artistic indignities, of Off-Off and Off Broadway to reach his goal—Broadway—he may find work at a living wage, but the work may be for only a few weeks at a time. And it has been thus for more than fifty years.

In mid-December of the 1972–1973 season on Broadway there were thirty-four legitimate theaters, sixteen of which were dark. Of the eighteen remaining, only a handful were taking in enough at the box office to make a profit. The formerly great Shubert chain, now including sixteen Broadway houses, had lost an aggregate of $2 million the previous season, and the Shubert organization, which included various nontheater enterprises, had suffered a net loss of half a million dollars—their first such loss since the Depression. Broadway was, as it had been season after season, in the grip of a confused pessimism. Under a recent city law designed to encourage the construction of theaters, four new theaters had been built and opened in the Broadway area—the first since 1928. But the problem was one of high cost of production, increased risk of failure and apparent scarcity of playwrights. During this period the highest-paid playwright in history, Neil Simon, continued to write and have produced comedy hits which, in Martin Gottfried's words, were not bad because they were funny, but because they were trivial.

The survival rates of shows were dismal. In the 1971–1972 season fifty-three shows opened; nine survived. Eighteen closed in the first three weeks. There were ninety-four Off Broadway openings, thirteen of which were still playing at season's end. And many shows never even opened—about forty aimed for Broadway and twenty-five for Off Broadway. With the cost of producing a play up to about $150,000 and the price tag of a musical at about $600,000, a total of about $25 million was spent in opening shows during that 1971–1972 season. One observer said the odds for making a buck were better with random betting at the race track than in backing a show.

In such an environment an actor spends most of his time *looking* for work. This was true in the 1940s, before television, when the routine was to haunt the agencies, auditioning for every open call listed in the trade papers, and trying to break into radio by doing commercials or "soaps," the daytime radio serials. With the advent of television, actors in radio moved over to this medium and out-of-work actors continued to seek work in commercials. This is not what the eager student hoped for, but doing a deodorant commercial would pay the bills till an opportunity to play Hamlet came along. (Often rather substantially—residuals can pay as high as $40,000 in one year for one commercial and a star may receive $250,000 per commercial.) Although the substantial income from "soaps" may be sought, this detour around theatrical activity is profoundly disheartening.

If the lucre of nontheater work attracts the actor, its lack of artistic value repulses him. The ardent ones stick to the theater rounds, eternally hopeful. But to work in professional theater is in many ways to have the worst of two worlds. If the break comes and a role in a Broadway play is landed, there are two possibilities: the show can hit, which means the actor may have to play that same role eight times a week for months or years; or it can flop, and the actor finds himself fired. A third possibility is available to an actor determined to beat the boredom of the long run: As soon as his play opens, he scurries to get agents and producers to come and see him so he can land a part in another show. This leads to rapid turnover in casts in shows where actors are not signed to run-of-the-play contracts. Off Broadway shows suffer because of this, but what else can an actor do who is trying to build a career in his profession?

In nonprofit theaters the actor is not much better off. Most nonprofit organizations keep a nucleus of acting staff, but also hire and fire as needed. The regional theaters frequently pay lower fees than New York theaters but they afford the actor a change of life-style and a chance to play in the classics.

The typical round for the actor involves nontheater odd jobs and Unemployment, playing individual short runs at the regional theaters, back to New York or to Los Angeles for film and television work to pay off debts and provide a small cushion for the next period of job hunting, a show job on a cruise ship to the Caribbean for a month or so, then beginning again at the beginning and endlessly retracing the circle until it is rarely broken with the house and pool near Hollywood.

The obvious question is: How can an actor keep or further develop the artistic skills needed for work in the theater in such a helter-skelter profession? It is necessary for musicians, dancers and singers to keep in constant practice and constant performance in order to sharpen the edge of their skills to razor keenness. The actor, too, must study, practice and perform to acquire and maintain his artistry. What happens to actors in long drought periods? Skills atrophy, competence diminishes, and with it, self-esteem and confidence.

The noted British director Peter Brook has made the point in his book *The Empty Space*, where he calls incompetence "the vice, the condition and the tragedy of the world theater on any level: for every good [work] there are scores of others . . . betrayed by a lack of elementary skills." According to Brook, who speaks for many professionals and critics on this, the basic techniques of staging, designing, speaking, walking across the stage, sitting, even listening, simply aren't sufficiently known. "Compare the little it takes," he says, "except luck—to get work in many of the theaters of the world with the minimum level of skill demanded say in piano playing: think of how many thousands of music teachers in thousands of small cities can play all the notes of the most difficult passages of Liszt or sight-read Scriabin. Compared with the simple ability of musicians, most of our work is at an amateur level most of the time. A critic will see far more incompetence than competence in his theatergoing."[5]

Clive Barnes has made the point in a different way, by comparing the constant practice and performance of dancers with actors. If actors, he has said, were to work a fraction of the amount of time that dancers do, the level of acting would be electrifying. The recognition of incompetence in actors has been widespread. Some have blamed insufficient preparation. But the poor actor, once launched into his so-called professional life, finds that most of his energies are spent away from the practice of his art. And the dark despair of the actor has been expressed by many performers of distinction, who describe the struggle in American theater as a hopeless one.

Margaret Webster, the last of an American dynasty of thespians reaching back 150 years to Ben Webster, called her second volume of memoirs *Don't Put Your Daughter on the Stage*. Discussing her book shortly before its publication in 1972, she firmly advised against entering the acting profession in America. Then sixty-seven years old, the dedicated actress said that classical theater just

5 Peter Brook, *The Empty Space*, London, Macgibbon and Kee, Ltd., 1968, p. 31.

"doesn't exist anymore. There is no place for anyone to learn it and there is no one to teach it." The death knell had been rung with the closing of the vaudeville houses, those little acting factories where performers could get experience. A further blow, she said, was the restriction by Actors Equity limiting the employment in America of English actors trained in the classical style. University and college drama departments, too, failed to cultivate conservatory, skill-oriented theater training. But the great problem was the profession itself. There is simply no way for actors to earn a living any more.[6]

This bleak reality has created a drain of theater professionals away from theater. They sometimes go into the film or television fields, or just leave. Alan Schneider, the Broadway director of Edward Albee's *Who's Afraid of Virginia Woolf?* and other successes, wrote stingingly of the problems of the professional in the legitimate theater in a perceptive article called "The Theater: Does It Exist?" He concluded that it was not surprising that "many more theater people than ever before, on all levels, are giving serious thought to leaving the theater." The reasons? They are unable "not only to bear the steadily intensifying vagaries (after all, the uncertainty is the one certainty of our profession), but [they are also] conscious of clearly and definitely shrinking opportunities, as well as the spread of mediocrity, amateurism, and madness almost in inverse proportion to the declining number of worthwhile works each season; confused by the ever menacing Babel of styles and approaches; wondering how much longer the mess can go on in the theater as it is going on outside the theater; they are for the first time in their lives facing a future outside of that profession to which they had at one time in a much different past given their emotional and physical selves.

[6] Margaret Webster, *Don't Put Your Daughter on the Stage*, New York, Alfred A. Knopf, 1972.

One day, it is an actor, reasonably well established and successful—whatever that means—but increasingly without roots, who meets me on the street and asks me for a smaller part in a play than he would have accepted a year earlier—and in the next breath wonders if I would like to get out with him and set up some sort of business: Portuguese ceramics? Antiques? Or, last summer, a serious young actor, in New York for more than ten years, writes a carefully thought-out piece in the *Times* on 'The Irrelevance of Being an Actor' in which he confesses to simple puzzlement, not to say bewilderment, at his growing inability to survive economically, or, more vital, spiritually. Or the founder of one of our more interesting regional theaters quits one day, without warning, in order to try his hand as a stockbroker because 'that's where the money is.' "[7]

Actors who quit the profession are one example of the drain. Those who move over to television or film are another. The solace for these media migrants is they *seem* to be engaged in acting. They are still before the public. They are seen in movie houses or on the home television set, and some of our best actors have become voice-overs in commercial-land. Orson Welles, for example, one of the finest American actors, has been using his great pipe organ of a voice to tell millions of television watchers to fly Eastern Airlines. Countless others have done the same. There is controversy over this practice among actors, however. Some say it is demeaning to the art; others say the money is good, and if that's the only way talent is to be recognized, then take the money. Few nonprofessionals have considered what this one-way street into film and television means to the legitimate theater, probably because few nonprofessionals are concerned about it. But many actors do recognize the differ-

[7] Alan Schneider, "The Theater: Does It Exist?," *Arts in Society*, Vol. 8 No. 3, University of Wisconsin, 1971.

ence between commerce and the art that attracted them to the field. Eli Wallach, a prominent stage actor who has also made films, has said with some bitterness, "What the hell! What's the use of struggling and being public spirited and all that when I can get $250,000 for three months' work on a movie."

The flow of actors from theater to film began early in the century when actors found the celebrity of film fame more seductive than the lesser fame of the stage. The Barrymores, Chaplin and countless stage professionals made films and their numbers increased when talking pictures were introduced in the late 1920s. The gradual siphoning off of talent has served to impoverish the theater, which still continues to serve film as a source of material and a training ground for talent. The quick rise to stardom of Dustin Hoffman in films such as *The Graduate* and *Midnight Cowboy* followed a brief period of work in small New York theaters, including the nonprofit American Place Theater. An actor can sometimes get a sense of artistic achievement from film work, but is this possible in the television commercials from which many actors make much of their money?

The well-known Irish actress Siobhan McKenna was once offered $100,000 to do a voice-over commercial. Miss McKenna made the point in an article in *The New York Times* that there was a moral issue involved. She argued that "One owes a duty to one's profession, and the public deserves to have dedicated actors and actresses unto themselves." Her view was disputed by an American actress, Maureen Stapleton.

Stapleton shot back, "A lack of money isn't particularly ennobling. In fact, I think it's soul destroying. Poverty is to me a crime, and it leaves irreparable scars." Miss Stapleton commented further on professional actors who took work on television comedy series, replying specifically to the charge by Miss McKenna about Shirley

Booth's having done a trivial comedy series called "Hazel." Although using an actress of Miss Booth's caliber for a long run of low situation comedy can easily be seen as an obvious despoiling of talent, Miss Stapleton defended the practice. "As for doing 'cheap television series,' Shirley Booth worked for years and years and years in the theater before she finally got the only chance an actor has to make some real money by having a successful, long-run television series." Once one has this bargaining position, according to Miss Stapleton, one can say "Drop dead to the witch doctor, but you can't say it when you haven't got two quarters to rub together."

Whether commercial work weakens the artistry of the actor or compromises his moral fiber varies according to the case. What is sure, however, is that the finest actors produced by Broadway and Off Broadway, once they enter film or television, are rarely seen in legitimate theater again. This causes a double impoverishment. Theater loses the cream of its acting talent as it is skimmed off, and actors risk losing their skills through loss of contact with the discipline of live performances. Unless the actor can balance electronic performance with stage work, artistry is sure to atrophy. In recent years this balance has been harder and harder to maintain as opportunities for legitimate theater work have declined and as the demand for and pay of the best actors to work in films and TV have soared. Consider this short list of actors who once brought life to the American stage and who now appear in legitimate theater irregularly, if at all: Orson Welles, Joseph Cotten, Ben Gazzara, Marlon Brando, Geraldine Page, Jo Van Fleet, Bette Davis, Katharine Hepburn, Shirley Booth, Sidney Poitier, Hume Cronyn, Jessica Tandy, Lee J. Cobb, George C. Scott, Eli Wallach, Anne Jackson, Walter Matthau, Jason Robards, Jr., Richard Widmark, Tony Curtis, Art Carney, Jonathan Winters, Mercedes McCambridge, Arlene Francis, Patty

Duke, Patricia Neal, Nina Foch, Gary Merrill, José Ferrer, Henry Fonda, James Stewart, Broderick Crawford, Dustin Hoffman, Al Pacino.

Often actors yearn so strongly for contact with their art that they seek a way back to theater themselves. Richard Chamberlain, who made his fame and fortune as young Dr. Kildare on a popular television series, took what for some would be a dangerous step when in 1971 he risked himself in a legitimate theater production of *Hamlet*. He did quite well.

Most English actors, with access to a superior theater system of regional houses doing classic repertory, are able to keep in artistic trim even while they make films. A notable example is Sir Laurence Olivier, who never stopped playing legitimate roles even though his film career was certainly the equivalent to that of any American star. And younger actors, too, having been trained in the classics, continue to keep in touch. Albert Finney, who attained international stardom in the film *Tom Jones*, had done his Hamlets and Cassios before, and after his film success he continued to work on the stage.

Among American actors who saw the need for stage work was the late Robert Ryan, who for years would go to England to work with theater companies there—at salaries far below his film income. Ryan joined with colleagues Martha Scott and Henry Fonda in 1968 in an attempt to operate a legitimate theater called the Plumstead Playhouse in Mineola, Long Island. (It subsequently moved to the Los Angeles area.) The venture was another indication that in America, the theater is subsidized by the actors. This trio felt that many established actors need to get back on stage and do great parts but they can't fit them into their film commitments.

It is no secret among theater professionals that something is drastically wrong. The central problem seems to be basically that of being an artist in a profession that strangles artistic effort both by limiting opportunity for artistic work in legitimate theater and by failing to offer wages commensurate with value received. The young actor is penalized in this system, and as the best young (and older) talents abandon the stage, they find it difficult to fit theater into their film or television commitments or, when they can, to find theater companies of high enough caliber to make working in them rewarding in artistic terms.

The realities of the acting profession not only have created a one-way street out of the theater, but have also tended to lower the self-esteem of the actor. Underpaid, underemployed, undervalued, even actors who have made the grade are susceptible to feelings of acute worthlessness.

Repeated failures take their toll. The feelings of rejection involved in the inability to get work, or having gotten it, in losing the job because the show closes, the indignity of following an artistic calling but being on Unemployment, contribute to a sickened psyche. The root cause is a lack of economic protection for the profession through adequate theater institutions. In American theater as presently constituted can there be any hope of raising the professional actor from his low state until the profession itself is given the dignity which a serious art form deserves?

To illustrate the problem of low self-image, and its relationship to the realities of the profession, here are a few examples. To Walter Matthau the need for success in theater was secondary to what he called a need to fail. This almost neurotic expression was conveyed in a *New York Times* interview with Matthau in which he spoke bitterly of the vanity of theater that only pretended to be cultural. Most actors, like himself, were trying to get roles in films, although a few preferred the purity of theater. He said he was shaped by humiliations and that this was healthier in an actor's development than success. It is an absurd point of view that perhaps can be understood as the poignant result of an actor's deprivation. That it is patently foolish, though, can be seen by applying the logic of the argument to another profession. Imagine a brain surgeon, for example, being tempered by failure and humiliation.

How often does one hear or read about the pleasure of acting? Not often. The emphasis is rarely on the contribution of the artist to society, but rather the lowest aspect of acting is stressed, and nowhere more regularly, fervently and perhaps even innocently than in the news media. Of all offenders in this respect none is worse than *The New York Times*, which maligns the profession with depressing consistency, even when it means to help!

When the *Times* is reviewing theater performances or interviewing members of the profession, there seems to be a hidden desire to cheapen and disparage. When its reporters write of nontheater matters the exploitation of actors can be downright degrading. A few examples:

A series of stories run in the paper was based on reports from one street, West Eighty-fifth Street between Central Park West and Columbus Avenue. Reporters cited problems on that block as case studies that might be typical of the wider city. One story was on Unemployment. Twenty-five residents of Eighty-fifth were receiving Unemployment checks, ten were named in the story, and the tenth was "an actor." Two photographs illustrated the story on the first page of Section II, one showing a dejected young man leaning on his elbow at a bare wooden table while staring blankly at a televised baseball game. The caption read: "Johnny Armen, an actor, feels 'residual middle class guilt' about receiving unemployment checks, but says that without them he couldn't be an actor." The other picture showed a glowingly healthy blond young woman with her bicycle. It was captioned:

"Carol Gordon rather enjoyed period of unemployment."
Miss Gordon was in advertising and publishing. No bias
against those fields.

Another story in the series was on love. The love-
situation for the entire block—perhaps the city—was
epitomized in a story of "a young woman from Wisconsin,
who *wanted to be an actress.*" She "moved onto the block
to save expenses and lived with an old friend, a homo-
sexual. Within a month, however, they were having an
affair, which went well, until he invited two other homo-
sexuals to share the apartment." It is, of course, gratuitous
to slur a profession by recounting the pecadillos of one
person who "wanted to be an actress."

A story illustrating the job of the New York civil service sheriffs and how they keep the city safe characterized
the actor as threat to society—again, gratuitously. "If an
actor is wanted for arrest," the story read, "a deputy may
not compel a theater manager to identify a member of
the cast. On the other hand, if the theater manager
refuses to cooperate, the deputy can pluck the actor off
the stage in the middle of the performance."

Not only the reportorial staff sees the actor as miscreant,
odd-jobber and bum. The cause of nonprofit theater was
upheld dubiously in a *Times* editorial about the APA-
Phoenix Theater and the New York Shakespeare Festival
Theater under the heading "Theatrical Beggars," in which
the two theaters were called "Those magnificent beggars
of Broadway and environs."

The trade paper *Variety* once caught the *Times* in an
unconscious act of degrading the actor in a story that
read, in part, "Alice Playten has been appearing in
'George M' at the Palace, N.Y., since last Oct. 14. She has
a small, unbilled role, but is receiving above-minimum
salary. A feature story in the Dec. 21 issue of the *N.Y.
Times* covered the actress-singer's career with emphasis
on the downbeat angles. The inescapable implication of

the piece to the uninformed reader was that she is currently unemployed. The fact that she's working steadily was not evidently deemed fit to print."[8]

Perhaps the *Times* only reflects a general societal attitude about the actor's worthlessness. But although the *Times* can distinguish a hoofer from a ballet dancer, a wedding band-musician from a concert artist, it makes no such distinctions in the theater profession. The actor playing the Fool in *King Lear* might be labeled a "comic," along with a night club entertainer. An "actress" can be a woman playing Hedda Gabler, or a stripper. Being an entertainer does not exclude the possibility of being an artist. But in a profession requiring great skill, considerable training and dedication to work, not to mention an above-average talent for projecting the subtleties of human behavior in dramatic contexts, distinctions should be made. It is essential that the critical faculties of those outside the profession be sharpened, especially those who inform and influence the public regarding the profession. Is it special pleading to wonder whether it was appropriate for the *Times* to carry a headline saying "Dog Actor Gets Aid for Hearing" over a story which began "Jake is a rising young actor"?

Fortunately for the continuation of the profession, the actor has learned to laugh at himself, although not too heartily. Frank Giordana wrote a satirical article for the *Times* entitled "What's It Like Being an Actor? I'll Tell You . . . ," and his view sums up what this chapter is all about.

"Being an actor," says Giordana, "is not being able to open a charge account at Bloomingdale's but signing for everything at Sardi's (and wishing Sardi's sold throw rugs and Spic and Span). . . . Being an actor is scrimping to keep up your union dues in the Actors Equity Associ-

[8] "Times Adds Pathos for Alice Playten," *Variety*, Jan. 1, 1971.

ation, the American Federation of Television and Radio Artists, and the American Guild of Variety Artists only to get an underwear commercial covered by the Screen Actors Guild, a union to which you do not belong and whose initiation fee is twice what you are going to make running around in those damn support hose for two days. . . . Being an actor is vowing that if you have to go through one more door marked 'OPEN CALL,' you would just as soon go through one marked 'OPEN WRISTS.' Being an actor is auditioning unsuccessfully for at least 150 commercials and trying to stifle two recurrent surrealistic nightmares in which A) you inflict bodily harm on Danny Thomas's real-life daughter, Terry, with a Maxwell House coffee jar, and B) you place a Roast and Boast bag over Eve Arden's head, leaving her chin deep in 'perfect gravy.' "

Actors yearn to act, to practice the art of theater. But where can that be done? When jobs come along, are they satisfying artistically to the actor, to the public? Seasoned actors want to play classic roles, and the young do, too. And they should, if they are to develop, to avoid the hopeless incompetence that stalks our stages. As young Robert Drivas said after a successful opening in Washington, D.C., as Hamlet, "They asked if I'd be willing to give up my lucrative television work to play Hamlet here for $100 a week. I said I'd *pay* the theater to play Hamlet."

In a profession where practice is grossly limited by a commercial system that values the new play above the actor, a noncommercial system that underpays and underachieves artistically, and a total system that underemploys and underpays, thus denigrating the very existence of the professionals, is there any wonder that the American actor finds himself on a one-way street? Or that American audiences are denied access to an art that could flourish in their cities if the profession were only granted the dignity it deserves and the professionals the opportunities and economic protection they seek and need?

When this one-way street was being paved in the early decades of this century, Theresa Helburn commented on the dubious, to her, pull of films. In 1929, after having spent a boring eight months in Hollywood as a script consultant where she was asked to render an opinion before having finished reading a script, she wrote, "The real artist in the theater is never, I believe, going to find full creative satisfaction in the movies. . . . Fine actors may be tempted by the money to forsake the theater for the pictures temporarily but they will inevitably come back with more relief and keener desire."[9]

She was, of course, absolutely right. And absolutely wrong.

[9] Theresa Helburn, *The New Republic*, Mar. 23, 1929.

3

A Royal American
Symphonic Theater

ONE WAITS IN VAIN for the return of the latest Broadway or Off Broadway talents who have graduated to films and television, the return Theresa Helburn so took for granted.

What kind of American theater could attract back the latest defectors? The theaters we have offered our best artists are playwrights' theaters on Broadway, where speculators bet on what will amuse large audiences for profit; and regional theaters, where high-flown rhetoric about artistic standards is belied by lack of attainment. We have no repertory theater, though experience has shown that repertory situations are healthy for actors. Brooks Atkinson has said that Americans do not like repertory theaters and don't want them; that they don't want to be uplifted, only entertained. But how can our actors grow in a self-destructive environment in which the greatest among them are forced to subsidize the theater—if they can find a theater whose standards are high enough to entice them to squeeze a stage role into their busy film-TV schedules?

Were we able to offer a challenge comparable to that of London's Royal Shakespeare or National Company, the loss of theater's luminaries would most likely be recovered. Since the millennium on Broadway is not around the corner, and since regional and nonprofit groups postpone large-scale commitments to a professional performers' company, I propose that we fill the vacuum—now—with the *Royal American Symphonic Theater*. *Royal* suggests the standards of excellence demanded for the benevolent and generous patronage that can lift our beleaguered profession from its current state. *American* implies the essential character of theater centers throughout the nation that are to include the world's heritage—of literature and its interpreters. *Symphonic* underlines the superior achievement and economic durability of our great musical institutions.

With a Royal American Symphonic Theater in each major city, millions of Americans would have access to a level of entertainment and amusement, of intellectual and emotional stimulation and social and political comment, now almost wholly absent from American life. An RAS Theater in each region might give America that barometer on which to register our country's greatness or its decline. Through its impact on film and television an RAS Theater system might raise the sensibilities of our people.

To accomplish this the RAS Theaters must be conceived and launched as battleships, unlike the little rowboats of our present regional theater. They should equal local athletic teams, symphonies, museums and universities—for example, the theater in Chicago should be as excellent as the Chicago Symphony, in Boston on a par with the great universities, in Los Angeles equivalent in importance and support to the Rams.

American cities have distinct personalities. Each RAS Theater must grow out of the needs and qualities of its home city and reflect the lives of the people it serves. Local ethnic cultures, economic and political considerations, industries and educational institutions should be expressed in the RAS Theater. And it must be organized around the best artistic leadership available. Sometimes that leadership is scarce in one city, and may have to be coaxed in—or back, in the case of the expatriate artist. In some cases the artistic leadership might choose a city. Whatever the formula, whether the theater is built on past work of local artists or on the visions of newcomers, the institution must revolve around the sun of a great artistic leader. As the symphony has its major-league conductor, so the theater must have nothing less than an equivalent theater artist at its head.

The annual budget of an RAS Theater might range from $3 million to $5 million or more, depending on its scope of operation and city of location, the expense of operation and the ability of the region to support it. The RAS Theater should offer the highest kind of theatrical entertainment and involvement possible. The seasons should be prodigious, with as many as forty plays produced during a year—classic tragedies and comedies, musicals, modern plays, experimental works, children's theater, puppetry, the whole gamut of theater. In order to embrace such a wide repertory many theater spaces would be engaged—perhaps nine or ten. The acting company should number about 100, with another 100 in technical staff, and each employee should be offered a living wage or better and reasonably long-term commitments. Within the company of 200 there should be permanent professional management, directors, stage managers and other production personnel, resident playwrights and *dramaturges*.

RAS Theaters would have to depend heavily upon subscriptions and donations and should therefore be locally organized specifically for subscribers. Subscription, I believe, is a measure of commitment, and without it no institution can long survive. Subscriptions need not be expensive and subscribers should be urged to see a play at least every two or three weeks during the season to develop the habit of theatergoing. The RAS Theaters should be true contemporary theaters. The value of the performer can be stressed in repertory theater, whereas in a theater where a long or limited run is the practice, the stressed value tends to be that of the play. There are times when the play *should* be the focal point, but since this has been the Broadway pattern that has so depressed the theater profession over the past fifty years, the concept of "the play's the thing" should be carefully reconsidered.

Repertory is not intrinsically a good idea; it must justify itself. In opera and ballet repertory is kind to performers who could not endure the physical demands of repeating strenuous roles. Most actors can repeat a role eight times a week, although this can lead to boredom and staleness. Running a play is not intrinsically a good idea either, though producers justify the practice economically: a play run for a long period at high prices reduces running costs and makes for high profits.

Rotating a repertory is the ideal system for actors. Besides the artistic justification for rotating repertory, there is an economic one. At first glance it would seem that rotating plays is too expensive because of the costs of handling the scenery. But such costs can be offset by an increased use of a particular theater space. A repertory company with only one performing facility can give as many as fourteen performances of several plays in one week without markedly increasing its basic overhead. Two separate theater companies, however, each giving seven performances of two plays each week is a more costly arrangement. But if one company has many theater spaces of varying size, the utilization of the largest houses—those apt to cost more to operate—in a rotating repertory system can allow for increased scheduling of space with the result being a less costly and more efficient operation in terms of using facilities and staff.

There are definite benefits to an audience of rotating repertory. RAS Theaters should appeal to the widest audiences in age and background. The repertory should reflect the desires and tastes of several audiences as well as management. I find the General Motors concept best: cars of different models, colors and prices are produced to appeal to the most number of people. The member of the local Kiwanis Club and a student radical are not likely to clamor for the same kind of play, but they should both be able to find what they want in the RAS Theater.

The policy of rotating repertory would also enable the RAS Theater to tailor to the audience's wishes the times of presentation: adult plays at night, children's theater in the mornings, matinees for older people. The guiding principle should be to offer the community *more* theatrical experiences than any one member would ever want, with the possible exception of the passionate theater lover for whom the stage is the center of human life— and praise be, there are a few of those in every community!

RAS Theaters should be designed for and located in communities other than New York City, for New York is the least likely place such a major theater could develop along the lines presented here. New York could doubtless profit from housing such a theater, but audiences in New York have what amounts to a comprehensive theater experience from the multiplicity of theater around town. Of course, the presence of these theaters has not brought about an improved profession, and no single New York theater offers to actors salaries or artistic work on a par with the New York Philharmonic or the Metropolitan Opera. But the sheer presence of so much theater activity in New York has probably persuaded professionals and community leaders that there is no need for an organization of this kind.

It is for other cities to create RAS Theaters, and it is my conviction that many of our cities could undertake this major theater experiment with deeply gratifying results. Being a New Yorker, however, I do hope that one day New York will have its RAS Theater, too.

4

Where the RAS Theaters
Might Grow

EVEN IN THE WORST of times, societies find ways to keep alive those institutions that improve their quality of life, and there is good reason to believe that over the long run the American economy will remain healthy. By this argument, many of our major cities qualify as capable of creating for themselves comprehensive theater institutions, since they already house notable arts institutions and other organizations that add important dimensions to human life.

Theater is and probably will continue to be of limited appeal. It is generally accepted that about 3 percent of a given population attends the performing arts. Granting that the fortunes of the theater, through subscription and donation, may rest on that small a percentage, it is still possible to project a successful funding. The task is to find the 3 percent and develop their interest.

If we estimate that a minimum of 30,000 subscribers would be needed to support an RAS Theater, there are quite a number of cities or Standard Metropolitan Areas that qualify.

There are many factors involved in finding the 3 percent, in then approaching the audience or audience groups that make up the total, in locating the theater or theaters in order to serve subscribers, in devising the appropriate schedule to satisfy the demands of the many varied interests.

Obviously, before any enterprise of large dimension is begun, careful planning must be undertaken. It is essential if a theater is to be founded that research precede planning. Research must indicate communication and transportation variables that would influence location of theater spaces. It must study diverse populations, what their interests are and what their theatergoing habits are, or could be. Audiences can be built by generating excitement on stage. But the theaters have to be located where the people can attend easily and safely.

The audience is like the balance wheel for the theater, complementing its action with reaction. The audience "finishes" the play, which does not become a play until words and actions are delivered from the stage to an audience. As an audience accepts or rejects a play or a policy, the artistic and economic life of the theater is shaped. If playgoers want trash, they will get it; if nourishment, that will be given. The artistic policy cannot be directed by the audience—it must be provided by the professional leadership. But the audience cannot be ignored.

The tastes of a potential audience must be researched, for that information will provide important clues to the theater's directors as to what can be done and whether an audience might be educable, and how far.

It isn't enough to survey only the quantifiables—population, distribution of wealth, habits of giving, predeliction for theater, education, leisure time. The imagination quotient has to be determined. What will an audience tolerate in the realm of the unfamiliar, the controversial? Will it merely put up with new forms, new values, or eagerly embrace them? Will it demand only Broadway reruns or classic plays or avant-garde theater? Since it has a creative role to play in the life of the RAS Theater, an audience must be capable of intellectual and emotional vitality.

An audience must include those with highly trained critical faculties. They can be professionals or valued amateurs who serve as gadflies to the theater's management. If an audience lacks articulation, the company may be unable to judge whether its work is reaching the intended levels of achievement. Arthur Miller once said that critics were for the public and not for artists, but that is not entirely true.

Critics should be knowledgeable. They should be connoisseurs capable of judgment based on scholarship. They should have insight into the nature of the artist and the creative process as well as a concern for the welfare of the audience. Good critics, like good playwrights or actors, are rare in any place or time. If local critics are below par, the organizers of an RAS Theater should suggest good critics to the local media. Since it is essential that the audience be able to communicate with the theater, it is important that a worthy critic be counterposed to the theater's management. Critical voices can help or hinder the life and growth of the theater.

If my premise is correct, that any city that supports major cultural, educational and athletic institutions can also host an RAS Theater, how many American cities have in fact been hospitable to theater, and to what extent? Seven of the twenty largest cities do have theater of some artistic quality. Population and per capita income do not seem to play as important a role in theater support as does desire for theater. For example, the Minneapolis–St. Paul urban area has an aggregate population of about 750,000, according to the 1970 census, ranking thirty-second among American cities. Yet the Twin Cities supported between them a major orchestra and a vigorous chamber orchestra, important art museums, universities, athletic teams and some twenty theaters, led by the doyen of American regional theaters, the Tyrone Guthrie. Minneapolis–St. Paul is not among the twenty most populous cities, but, after New York, it has more theaters than any other city in America.

The exceptional example of this medium-sized urban area makes it possible to assert that the critical 3 percent can be found in many American cities—and around them as well. The Guthrie pulls subscribers from as far away as 700 miles!

The seven theater-supporting cities in the top twenty are, in order of population, New York, Los Angeles, Houston, Washington, D.C., Cleveland, Milwaukee and San Francisco. New York has more theaters than all the others combined. What do the other large cities have— Chicago, Boston, Detroit, Philadelphia, Pittsburgh, St. Louis? Small regional theaters, community theater, some experimental groups, dinner theaters, Broadway road companies.

The existence of theater is a matter of choice and perhaps chance, and, in some cases, propinquity. Little New Haven has for decades had a theater consciousness. Near New York, it was ideal for pre-Broadway tryouts and welcomed theater. Perhaps as a result of this climate the Long Wharf Theater has grown to be one of the most important regional theaters and can develop a new play and even transfer it to New York, as was the case with *The Changing Room.* The Yale Repertory Theater in New Haven has also won artistic distinction with its productions.

Though desire and climate for theater must be reckoned more important than population or per capita income, these two factors will play a key part in launching an RAS Theater. Population figures, however, can be misleading because of the patterns of city growth. American cities have been changing in varying ways with differing rates of change. We assume that cities tend to lose population, but from 1960 to 1970 eight of our largest cities gained population (twelve lost). More important, some of the gainers grew markedly, while in the losers the drop was only fractional. Indianapolis, the eleventh largest city in 1970, grew at a rate of 56.6 percent from 1960 to its 1970 total of 745,739 people. Increases were also shown in the following cities (in order of percentage increase): Phoenix, Houston, Memphis, Dallas, San Diego, Los Angeles and San Antonio.

Statistics showing population loss can also be misleading because a city limit is merely a political boundary that fails to describe the people who relate to the city for work, services and leisure. People leave central cities to find more room, better housing, better schools, a better esthetic environment. From ancient times until today the rule of thumb has been that workers are willing to commute about an hour from home to place of work. Distance is calculated in commutation time, not miles. In the 1880s Detroiters moved out of the center of the city to a distance an hour away by horse and buggy. Today the distance that can be traveled in one hour—by car or train —is much greater. But the city limits tend to remain set, even though the communities surrounding and sometimes joining neighboring cities together form corridors of transportation and communication around and between cities and represent the real city limits. For example, all the big cities of Ohio "lost" population during the 1960s, but the state gained by 9.7 percent. Cleveland lost 14.3 percent and nearby Akron 5.1 percent, but the chances are the "lost" population now lives in the corridors between. The same is probably true for Toledo and Detroit.

In order to deal with the audience-population question it would be well to pair nearby cities and take a reading of the aggregate population included in the interstices. If good transportation arteries exist, a clearer picture of potential audience may be indicated. For example, there are some 1.2 million people living in and between Dallas and Fort Worth and they are well enough served by highways so that a theater advantageously located could be easily accessible to either city and the in-between communities by car.

Seattle and Everett, Washington, have an aggregate population of about 1.4 million—more than enough to provide the 30,000 subscribers needed for the theater. San Francisco, Oakland and Berkeley, California, have a metropolitan area population of 3.1 million. The Los Angeles-Long Beach area contains more than 11 million people.

In the search for the potential audience the accent should be on the Standard Metropolitan Area (SMA) rather than the city, as understood in terms of legal boundaries and census figures. Only six American cities have more than 1 million inhabitants. But the metropolitan area charts show that twenty-one SMAs have more than 1 million; three of those have more than 5 million and nine have between 2 and 5 million.

One workable definition of an SMA's limits would be the range of the local television news coverage and signal—usually from fifty to sixty miles in radius. Drawing from this kind of radius and assuming rapid transportation to and from the RAS Theater, an audience attending a show at 8 P.M. could be home by midnight.

Boston, America's sixteenth largest city, had only 641,071 people in 1970, with a decrease of 8.1 percent suffered in the 1960s. But taking in the surrounding communities, the total metropolitan area exceeds 2,750,000. This total area supports and is served by Boston's fine museum, great universities, one of the world's finest symphony orchestras—the Boston Symphony—major athletic teams, the innovative Opera Company of

Boston, some budding dance companies, but no major theater. A ripe city for an RAS Theater.

Southern cities might be promising sites for professional theaters. Although Northern cities lost population in the 1960s, a pattern of increase was noted in the South. Nashville, Tennessee, and its neighboring city of Davidson had a 30 percent rise in population, from 170,874 in 1960 to 447,877 in 1970. The rise of Nashville as a major source of commercial recording has brought an influx of musicians and other professionals to that community. Florida continues to grow at a rapid rate and the high cost of oil and other energy fuels may spur more migration southward.

The one-sided system whereby the arts were patronized heavily by only wealthy families has diminished somewhat, although it has by no means vanished. But the arts patron from the smaller income brackets is a fairly recent fact of life in America and should be developed.

If research shows that audiences and support exist for an RAS Theater, one must remember that it is folly to construct a facility before an organization has been formed to occupy it. The motto should be: "Build to Suit Tenant." If there is no tenant, wait. In several communities, including New York City, organizations have made the mistake of planning construction and actually putting up a building before there was a company to run it. A spate of theater construction followed the opening of Lincoln Center in 1962, and the guesswork has produced spotty results. Leaders in this continuing flood of activity are colleges, universities, junior colleges and high schools, all interested in putting up concert halls and theaters. Municipalities and regional governments are financing theater construction too. Attendance at American civic centers over the country in 1966 for cultural attractions was more than 260 million. In 1967 more than $100 million was slated to be spent by the nation's cities in construction. These included new halls for concerts, which often also provided space for local amateur theaters, community theaters or Broadway plays on tour.

An example of how one community handled its planned expansion in the arts is the case of Norfolk, Virginia. It has built a Cultural Convention Center comprising two spaces, a 2,800-seat theater with a 250-seat experimental or rehearsal space. There was not, nor is there yet, a professional theater company. Town fathers, however, saw the Cultural Convention Center as "strategic" to a downtown urban renewal project. The name implies the multiple concept and use of a general space. Norfolk got help from the federal government under the 1965 Federal Housing and Urban Development Act to rejuvenate the decaying center-city. Their reasons for construction were: (1) to aid specific sectors of the local economy, (2) to increase the cultural life of the community, (3) to help carry on civic affairs requiring meetings of large numbers of people and (4) to add to the total attractiveness of the area in the hopes of stimulating economic development.

Funds for such construction can be attracted from outside a community, since an esthetically stimulating project can increase tourism, improve the image of a city and attract new industry and businesses. The queen of American cultural centers, Lincoln Center, has brilliantly led the way in this as well as in other respects. In ten years of existence the travertine marble halls of Lincoln Center and its great plaza, fountain, park and band shell transformed a former West Side slum into a booming real estate area. It has been estimated that the value of the surrounding acreage in the Lincoln Center area has appreciated by more than $700 million—with a consequent $30 million increase in tax revenues for New York City.

The cardinal sin was committed against theater by

Lincoln Center, however. The Vivian Beaumont Theater was designed and built at the same time the now-defunct Lincoln Center Repertory Theater was being assembled. The result was a far from ideal theater space in which the repertory needs of the company were badly misjudged.

As important as it is to find the audience, it is equally important to be able to attract leading performers to the theater. For this reason, founding an RAS Theater in any particular city will to some extent be related to artists' willingness to work in that city for long periods. Cities might be ranked by charm, esthetic appeal, high standards of living and reasonable living costs, climate, style of architecture, atmosphere, educational facilities and a number of other civic, financial, cultural and societal features in order to determine their attractiveness to artists. Theater actors tend to want to stay near the centers of their other markets—television and film production (New York and Los Angeles are the two concentration points for film and television work)—but jet travel puts both within a few hours from most American cities.

Assuming either a city has decided to undertake the establishment of an RAS Theater, or the organizers have selected a city for such establishment, it is essential, as previously stressed, to find that audience the theater will address itself to. It can and should be a large and varied audience. Once this has been done, the theater must commit itself to that audience, to that community, not only through its performances, but also through its recruitment and hiring of personnel. It might be difficult or impossible to choose artists from the community, since the best talents will have already left for places where opportunities exist. But production personnel should be recruited from communities, with special attention paid to providing employment opportunities for ethnic minorities. Once assembled, the theater's staff should participate in community activities. The theater should mirror to a large extent the community's own self-image. Whether theater spaces are chosen downtown, or in a suburb, or on a campus, or in these and other places simultaneously, the placement of theater spaces constitutes another kind of community commitment. And location will help, through development of specific local audiences, to shape the theater's profile.

Campuses continue to offer hospitable conditions for theaters. The University Resident Theater Association (URTA), a national organization of collegiate theater professionals and academicians, sought in 1972 to link theater activity to the teaching of the humanities, a further tie between performance and scholarship that is strengthening the position of theater professionals interested in working on campuses, who were previously discouraged by what was a rigid academicism regarding performance practice and the relation of the performing arts to scholarship and curriculum. Robert Schnitzer, then head of the three-year-old URTA, said that such institutional affiliation would provide a basis for a more secure administrative life and therefore a better artistic operation.

An enthusiastic and loyal audience is the heart of the economic security of the subscription system. The critic, Julius Novick, describes the establishment of regional theaters around America in his book, *Beyond Broadway*, as ventures that began as acts of faith. Their founders didn't know until they tried whether their cities had the audience potential to support theater. In the beginning there was a euphoric period of excitement when backers and artists were one in confidence. Then the money people eventually realized that although they had found enough money to *start* a theater, they could not raise enough to maintain one. Euphoria over. The board of directors, knowing it must meet the rising deficits, and that the audiences which were attracted to the novelty of the venture were no longer coming, would meet in near panic. Sometimes the theaters were closed, sometimes the artistic directors were fired for this or that reason, sometimes activity was curtailed. Long-term efforts at audience building, however, had failed, and that was generally a key to the crises. A theater space might have proved to be disastrously uneconomic. In a city of 2 million with a ball park holding 40,000, the theater might seat only 800 people at a play!

Although I have suggested that subscribers will probably come from the 3 percent of a given population that is normally supportive of the performing arts, I would now like to alter that concept and broaden it. Basing a theater on this 3 percent may be realistic, but every effort must be made to enlarge the community of theatergoers. To begin with, the obvious supporters of theater should be recruited. Studies have shown that in the total urban population performing arts audiences come overwhelmingly from professional people—about 62 percent; teachers, managerial and clerical workers make up about 15 percent of the total audiences and blue-collar workers about 5 percent, with students making up the balance.[1] Traditional attenders can be attracted in familiar ways. Sir Tyrone Guthrie lamented the need to mix the artistic aspirations of the theater with middle-class social climbing through the chic opening night, but he recognized its power of attraction. The sense of occasion, which was one of the most valuable stock-in-trade items in theater, was what television by its very nature found impossible to achieve and what film has tried again and again to capture, without success. The only thing wrong with the opening night "occasion" is that it reinforces the idea that

[1] Bowen and Baumol, op. cit.

theatergoing is elitist—a "have" experience denied to "have-nots." But I think the flamboyant glamor and frivolity can project the theater into the consciousness of a community with agreeable speed.

If the theater's promotion and publicity campaigns are aimed at the most accessible group of theater supporters in the beginning, it should pragmatically be in order to form a nucleus around which to develop the larger audience. A determined effort to broaden the initial group, to invite all into the club, will mean that the 3 percent must be broadened, too. The indifference of various groups must be penetrated. A church's minister should be invited to performances to scout the experience for his parishioners. Union and other blue-collar worker representatives should be invited in too. Leaders of social, ethnic and labor groups should be contacted by the theater.

The staff must keep in close touch with the realities of the community's entertainment habits and expectations —what's on television, in the movies, at athletic events. Ticket prices must be competitive. Children must be considered. A great failure in audience building, after the initial nucleus is formed and a supportive subscription list developed, is neglecting to step up efforts at audience recruitment in periods of success. No matter how well a season is going, there will always be empty seats. An example is the Metropolitan Opera, which under Sir Rudolf Bing had some success in selling itself to the public and finished many seasons having played to 97 percent capacity houses. But that management realized it could not relax, since the empty 3 percent of the seats amounted to some 30,000 unsold seats a season. Filling those 30,000 seats was an enormous job!

A theater can go to a community in a variety of ways. One study done on audience building in Minneapolis stated that among theater projects for nontheatergoers could be "programs of Bible readings for churches, appropriate presentations for union halls and programs of readings, scenes, and songs for the 4-H, Kiwanis, PTA's, and Lions Clubs, all by actors from the theater."[2]

Dogged work by public relations teams and inspired readings by actors around the community is important, but it would be as wrong to credit full houses to these efforts as to blame empty ones on lack of them. A good press agent may be able to increase audiences to some extent, but what makes audiences come is great performers in exciting, entertaining, stimulating theater in an area where an audience for that kind of theater exists. The quality contact with the audience is essential. Audiences tend to respond to a clearly expressed intention to seek a high level of performance even though the theater has not yet reached that level. Aspiration counts. Potential is rewarded. The best public relations image is that of a theater where things are happening, a place to return to, the place to be. An audience must feel a sense of promise of excitement as it approaches the premises and enters the theater.

A bright note in our recent history has been the increased awareness among Americans of the value of the arts, and the rising demand on the part of the people to have access to the arts and participate in them. This process of democratization of the arts, so recent in America, has also been a recently growing phenomenon in such presumably arts-conscious countries as England. Sir Hugh Millat, secretary general for the Arts Council of Great Britain, said in 1972 that if the arts in England were to have a proper economic base and a right position in society, more money would have to be effectively steered in the right directions, namely into publicity, promotion and new administrative structures for the arts.

In 1962, when America's dormant arts consciousness

[2] Bradley G. Morison and Kay Fliehr, *In Search of an Audience*, New York, Pitman Publishing Corp., 1968, p. 212.

was only beginning to awaken, Sir Tyrone Guthrie looked around the country for a place to build a theater and decided, happily, on Minneapolis. Among the factors influencing his decision was his preference to be a big fish in a smaller pond, which convinced him *not* to locate in New York. At that time, in 1962, the plans for the Lincoln Center Repertory Theater were receiving much excited attention in the press. Guthrie was dubious about Lincoln Center, but cautiously optimistic about theater outside New York, although he said that America's provincial cities might have to content themselves with "festivals" rather than true theater.

But the new attitude toward the arts has made the country more amenable to the creation of arts organizations of a broad character. The conditions are now ripe for great theaters in American cities; it is only the desire to develop them that is needed.

5

Assembling the RAS Theater Company

THE MOST VISIBLE ASPECTS of a theater are its company and playing spaces, for they proclaim what the theater is about. All decisions relating to these two areas are crucial to the realization of artistic goals. With weak actors, the best attempts to create artistic excitement will be hopelessly frustrated. Remarkable performances have taken place in unlikely and ugly theaters, but the most beautiful theater has yet to save a poor performance.

There may be relatively few actors who could join an RAS Theater, but they exist and they must be scouted, coaxed, enticed, pressured into joining. Under no circumstances should there be auditions for company members. Democracy has nothing to do with the vision of an artistic director.

Lest the no-audition policy seem unreasonably harsh, consider the absurdity of present theater auditions. They are both laughable and pitiful. Merely announce open auditions for a play and a line will form around the block of amateurs, professionals and aspirants just off the bus from Davenport, Iowa. But announce that a position as last chair violist in the Boston Symphony is open, and what happens? Will the amateurs flock? Of course not. The same is true in ballet. Only in theater are the standards so low that the unskilled and untrained dare compete for professional work.

From ten to twenty of the projected hundred company actors must be top professionals hired on short-term contracts and at reasonably high salaries. This nucleus will enable the theater to reach artistic heights quickly and demonstrably. Within flexible repertory limits, actors should be offered roles that they yearn to play or challenges that they had not considered.

There are many examples of name actors taking limited-run engagements for artistic reasons. In its final season the Lincoln Center Repertory Theater brought in actors such as Hume Cronyn and Jessica Tandy and the director Alan Schneider to do some virtuoso turns in a series of short plays by Samuel Beckett: *Krapp's Last Tape, Happy Days, Not I* and *Act Without Words*. The plays were familiar to New York critics and audiences, and attention was rightly focused on the brilliance of the performances. Walter Kerr wrote in *The New York Times* that audiences may have seen the plays but "what audiences have *not* been able to see, however, is Jessica Tandy and Hume Cronyn up to their necks in sanddunes or snarling at tape-recorders. They've seen other admirable performers . . . tackle the Beckett despairs and humors born of those despairs, but they really don't know what particularly savage insights or unexpected colors of voice Miss Tandy and Mr. Cronyn might have whirling about, waiting for release, in their heads. And *that's* a good reason for having this kind of theater: an actor's reason that becomes an audience's reason for going back again and again." In this case the "actor's reason" was the desire of Tandy and Cronyn to do what they could, and do it superlatively.

Another example was the production of Chekhov's *Uncle Vanya*, mounted by the Circle in the Square in its 1972–1973 season, in which George C. Scott and Nicol

Williamson headed a cast of notables. Such stars have time and again indicated a desire to work in legitimate theater, but their busy film schedules often prevent their doing so. In order to have a George C. Scott perform with a theater, it will be necessary to begin planning a year or two in advance. Such actors should be invited to join an RAS Theater company on whatever basis is mutually acceptable. The theater's organizers would have to form a team constantly to observe theater, television and film in order to keep up with the activities and whereabouts of our best acting talents. These individuals should be contacted and, prior to the organization of the theater, commitments should be obtained regarding their participation. It may take considerable enticement to lure actors from other theaters, film or television, or even out of retirement. The best kind of enticement would be the challenge to create, along with the founders, an American theater company of international distinction.

Although the nucleus may have to be enticed, with the announcement in the press of such a major theater venture many actors below the star category would probably express an interest in joining. Professional actors in regional theaters who have reached a plateau of artistic growth and need new experiences, new challenges, would want to join. In some cases the RAS Theater may wish to look to other theaters for personnel.

In addition to recruiting individuals, or allowing individuals who express an interest to join, other theater groups might be asked to join the company in toto. A small avant-garde troupe or an exciting ethnic theater company could be important wings of the theater. Experimentalism and expressions of the new sense of ethnicity in America are important aspects of the total artistic program of any major theater. For example, a black company in the city of location might benefit from working with the theater's artists, and the theater would benefit from the heightened social awareness the black company could bring to audiences. And nonwhite actors should, of course, be invited to develop their talents by taking on the great classic roles. New directorial interpretations have rendered polyethnic casts commonplace.

The diverse elements would add spice and variety to the theater's total style. The uniqueness of the RAS Theater company should be the gathering under one institutional management of talented performers from all aspects of theater and concentrating their talents in bringing the art of theater to one community.

It is not as important for the RAS Theater to have a catholic point of view, however, as it is to emphasize artistry, craft and skill. All professional types should be represented by significantly talented and skilled performers. Regardless of a vogue for amateurism (exemplified in the rise of director Tom O'Horgan, whose Broadway productions of *Hair* and *Jesus Christ, Superstar* elevated the hippie to professional actor), there should be no place for nonacting in a RAS Theater. The company should establish a relationship with a school of drama that will prepare students to meet the professional standards of RAS theaters. As an outlet for the energies of members of the company who are also gifted as teachers, school and theater will derive mutual benefits, akin to the relationship that exists between the Curtis Institute of Music and the Philadelphia Orchestra.

Once the company proves its artistic worth, it may become a professional goal for serious performers—in fact, it may not be able to absorb the number of talented actors who ask to join. Though there might be initial resistance on the part of some established actors to join a new company, once it has established its artistic reputation, a performing credit with the company would be of value to an actor. This would especially attract younger performers and the theater would benefit from gaining a reputation as a prime training ground and place of exposure for new talents. Actors would benefit through the increased attention paid them by producers who could offer opportunities that might include entrée to a Broadway success, for Broadway will continue to exert its force on American theater and one cannot deny its allure.

In the RAS Theater, repertory should be as important as the development of an ensemble style, and one might lead to the other. The fact that actors would be employed for long periods in a variety of plays would tend to develop ensemble playing. Constant employment is a key to maintaining skill. Ensemble style, however, which has its own inner dynamics apart from the demands of a particular play, is not achieved merely by keeping the actors busy. It requires working under a unified concept of direction. Since ensemble should be secondary, holding the company of actors together for long periods is not really essential. There are ways, though, to encourage long-term affiliation with a company if that is desirable. Kenneth Tynan, the British producer-director, has pointed out that the best way to guarantee an actor's continued presence in a company is by allowing him the freedom to come and go on a regulated basis. Ensemble theater is egalitarian; classic theater is feudal or monarchic. The RAS Theater must cast its plays as meticulously as a major Broadway production does. Very few repertory companies, university companies, regional theaters —no matter what they say—actually do. The Broadway method of producing for the opening night (sometimes called "festival" producing) results in a high level of achievement, albeit for a short time. But as National Theater director Peter Hall once said, "The only way you'll get actors to stay in a permanent company, in our Western society, is by letting them go. Then they'll come back." If an RAS Theater production depends on one actor, who must take time off after a short run, the schedule must be flexible enough to absorb the loss.

When the company is presented to the public in a play, the order of billing becomes important, for billing is a result of concept. The announcement of a star's name will attract interest. But should that name be placed above that of the play? In repertory, the company's billing policy should be to list all members of a cast alphabetically. The concept that should be plain to the public is: All the actors are equally important (the public will make its own stars). If the policy is to advertise certain parts, then whoever plays those parts will be featured. Curtain calls should likewise be arranged in order of importance of the role, not the celebrity of the actor. If Miss X is brought in at some expense to play a cameo role in a play, she should take her curtain call and be billed according to the importance of her role. Some actors will fight this, but the breaking of the merit pattern can cause more trouble than fighting to keep it. If an exception is made, it must be done in full knowledge that more may be lost than gained in doing so. Defeat of policy must be justified only by artistic quality—or survival.

One of the great operatic artists is Birgit Nilsson, the magnificent Swedish soprano. And yet Nilsson's name always appeared in the N's in the Metropolitan Opera's roster of artists according to a set formula. When Helen Hayes was a member of the now defunct APA-Phoenix Theater her name was listed alphabetically among the cast; but when the theater toured Kelly's *The Showoff* to raise funds her name was placed above the play's. The venture made some money, but the theater company died. When a company abandons a company ideal, it may also abandon its reason for existence.

6

Choosing the Repertory

THERE ARE SOME 2,000 summaries of plays "judged to possess some literary merit" in the four-volume McGraw-Hill *Encyclopedia of Drama* and new plays are being written every day. This embarrassment of riches, derived from over two thousand years of theater in the East and West, is the mother lode which the RAS Theater will mine. How to choose?

What are the criteria for balancing new and classic plays? Repertory will affect all aspects of the theater. The actor is trained by what he plays. And the stature of actors and directors is measured by those plays called "classic." Audiences develop their discriminatory skills in the classic repertory.

If a company is to develop toward its peak aspirations, it must concentrate on the classics, for that is where it must excel. If the standard is equalled, there is little the company cannot do. How well can the company perform Shakespeare? How well can this or that actor bring to life the classic roles? These are severe tests for the company, and the artistic direction must put the company through such tests, and the actors must pass them. Shakespeare must be taken on substantially, along with other major playwrights.

There is no reason to believe that unfamiliar classics will fail to attract new audiences. On the contrary, the RAS Theater should assume that a public exists for the unknown as well as the known classics—a public whose tastes are higher than what the mass media showmen would have us believe. All my experience indicates that there are enough patrons to make good theater artistically and economically feasible. The theater, then, should address itself to finding that audience from the beginning. It should, therefore, found its policy on a core repertory of classic plays brilliantly cast and performed. With the foundation of this repertory, both the company and the audience can be built together.

Antonin Artaud, the great French director, would dispute this approach perhaps, for he loudly protested as the greatest enemy of vital theater the contemporary middle-class notion of "art." Artaud said, "No more masterpieces," and Robert Brustein has echoed and amplified his battle cry by saying that tolerating the classics is not valid unless the performances have the power and immediacy of living experience. Brustein believes the audience should rebel against the "piety reflected in the very word 'masterpiece.' "[1] And this is precisely the point: What musician would tolerate a performance of a Wagner masterpiece if it were not vital? Why should standards for theater classics be low? Although a play may have great literary merit, its true value may be only perceived in a great performance.

The latitude for choice is so wide within the context of the classic literature that there is ample room for expression of individuality for each RAS Theater. In order to project a coherent artistic policy the overall artistic statement should be made via the repertory in a way discernible to the public. True, the theater that is not closely

[1] Robert Brustein, "No More Masterpieces," *Yale Theater Magazine*, Spring 1968.

wedded to its own time tends to become decadent, a mouthpiece for parochial or elitist values only. But this does not mean that only contemporary plays must be done. There are numerous ways of reinterpreting the classics so as to throw light upon current situations. Indeed, much of what is happening in our society has been anticipated in past plays. What *coup d'état* does not pull a leaf from *Julius Caesar* or *Richard II*?

Major themes and programs should emerge from the season's plays. Artistic themes can be developed by scheduling seasons of history plays, classic plays with topical relevance, plays giving a profile or even deep exposition of this or that national school—the theater of France, Germany, Italy, Russia, England, the Scandinavian countries. Single major playwrights might be treated to retrospectives over several seasons. And with a season of more than thirty plays there is room for minor themes. Are the plays of Shakespeare finite in their interpretations? So many approaches have been tried—multiple casting of *Hamlet*, a rock 'n' roll *Hamlet*, a modern-dress *Macbeth*, a Haitian *Macbeth*, a circus version of *Midsummer Night's Dream*—that the possibilities seem endless. Perhaps an artistic goal would be to develop a contemporary view of the Shakespeare plays, or another body of work, and that point of view might in itself be a contribution to the development of theater. A company might do the same play in two radically different interpretations, using different actors, sets and costumes, just for the sake of contrast. Although such an experiment might be too sophisticated at the outset, when the company is fully developed it should be able to do it successfully.

A systematic survey of various schools of theater would help the company broaden its skills and give the audience a more comprehensive experience. A repertory of black theater works could form one program of a theater in most of our cities through a survey of the literature by such important black writers as Langston Hughes and the Harlem Renaissance writers, and the moderns— Lorraine Hansberry, Ed Bullins, Imamu Amiri Baraka (LeRoi Jones), Ron Milner, Oyamo, Walter Jones, Richard Wesley, Charles Gordone, Melvin Van Peebles, Joe Walker and others. And there would be room for the new playwrights, too. Playwrights continue to be the voices of theater and they must have a prime role in any new theater undertaking. The theater should not only be willing to develop the new play, but, more importantly, the playwright. This is done not by looking for a winning play, producing it and running it to make money, which is the Broadway system, but by working with a playwright over a long period of time, allowing his new works to be tested in small-audience houses where he can rework them or possibly throw them away. Betting on the playwright, rather than on the individual play, would be a great contribution to the future of theater.

For example, Arthur Miller chose to have his play *The Creation of the World and Other Business* done on Broadway. The play ran forty performances during the 1972–1973 Broadway season, then closed. It had followed the usual pattern of a four-week rehearsal period leading to an out-of-town tryout run, during which actors and actresses were replaced, a director resigned and all the mishaps that can occur to a Broadway-bound show did, each taking its toll in terms of the playwright's time and ability to ready the play for its opening. At the opening the play's weaknesses were unattended to, most of the playwright's time having been spent elsewhere. An ideal situation would have been for Miller to entrust his new play to a company that would have worked with him on its production over whatever period of time was needed to achieve the desired artistic result—four weeks, six weeks, six months, a year.

The new playwright needs the same kind of opportunities the established artist needs—even more so—opportunities which are most rare in American theater.

If it is decided to do a new play on the basis of its own themes and needs, all those requirements that cost the playwright dearly in the Broadway or Off Broadway system would be met immediately and without difficulty. The relationship between playwright, director and producer would be purer. The writer would not have to rely on a speculative producer making decisions based on potential investment return rather than artistic results. The major theater would survive the "failure" of a new play simply because it would be organized to absorb projected deficits and not rely wholly on box office for its operation. In fact, the "failed" play could receive added work time and possibly be presented successfully in a revival. The theater could provide the necessary ingredients for the realization of the playwright's intentions. He would have at his play's disposal fine actors, directors, designers, production facilities, plus the willingness of all to attain his artistic goal.

But if the theater eliminates the weaknesses and drawbacks of the Broadway system, the "pot o' gold" dream need not be completely relinquished. Why couldn't a successful play, which had promise of making money, be given an extended run, perhaps a tour? This complex question would have to be decided by management as one of the basic guidelines for the theater. But the excitement of the new play and of developing a new playwright is a value of the highest order. A Broadway production, even if it is a hit, may be dead in two years or so. But if a play stays in a company's repertory for five years, that is worth something to a playwright, who wants the life of the play and not merely the money. The RAS Theater would be able to offer this life.

Musicals should, of course, form a part of the theater's

repertory. They use large casts and therefore greatly increase production expense, but they are also popular and would generate income.

American arts organizations rarely make a place for children. The RAS Theater should have an important children's theater: not condescending plays for children, but exciting theater involving them as participants. Children's theater in America is generally weak, but there are bright spots as models: the Paper Bag Players of New York, the Academy Theater of Atlanta, the Trinity Square Playhouse of Rhode Island and the Minneapolis Children's Theater.

Interest in children's theater has been rather low in professional circles. At the Fourth Biennial Congress of the International Association of Theater for Children and Youth, held for the first time in America in June 1972 at the State University of New York at Albany, there was practically no theatrical press coverage, even though several important foreign companies were visiting these shores for the first time. Of those foreign troupes that scored huge successes in Albany—and the Central Moscow Children's Theater's lavish production of a Soviet version of *Snow White* played to an enthusiastic audience at the Saratoga Performing Arts Center—not one was invited to stay and perform after the congress. This would seem to support the accusation that the professional theater ignores the benefits of creative drama as educational and social tools and as a base for theater training even while it loudly bemoans its shrinking audiences.

The theater's repertory should also include puppetry. America's recent growth of interest in puppetry has secured a new place for this perenially popular art form. Puppetry has a distinguished lineage in Western and Eastern cultures and some of its present practitioners continue to vitalize its traditions. Television has had major puppet theaters, with *Howdy Doody* in the 1950s, *Kukla, Fran and Ollie* and the *Sesame Street* "Muppets" of the late 1960s. One of the most distinguished of America's legitimate theater puppeteers is Bil Baird, whose Bil Baird Marionettes have played in their own theater in New York for several decades. In his book, *The Art of Puppetry*,[2] Baird traces the history of this art from its roots in ritual down to the present, and reviews his own experiences in forty years as master puppeteer. In it is much valuable advice on his art.

The inclusion of various types of theater should be accomplished under the unifying principles of the theater's artistic goals and policies. Those policies can be avowedly social or ideological. Eugene Ionesco feels that ideology is out of place in a work of art, but some directors openly espouse it. It is legitimate to hold either point of view. An example of an ideological impetus in theater was the 1971 production by sixteen major West German theaters of Peter Weiss's new play *Hölderlin*. This play about the nineteenth-century poet was clearly a pro-Marxist effort and each of the sixteen theaters gave a differing production which underlined this or that political or social twist. The Weiss marathon was not unusual in Germany.

In 1972 Robert Brustein was concerned about the lack of experimentation with the classics in repertory theaters in Great Britain. Successful, these repertory theaters seemed "momentarily stalled." Brustein asked the question: "Is the repertory goal to be reached by choosing the safe and routine or by testing untried formulas? Should the repertoire of a provincial theater be essentially regional—local plays about local problems—or should it include more general themes and universal considerations? Is it a theater's obligation to turn out anthology

[2] Bil Baird, *The Art of Puppetry*, New York, Macmillan, 1965.

plays in textbook productions, or should it be commissioning new works, unearthing neglected works of the past and exploring contemporary avenues into the familiar masterpieces? To whom does the theater owe its primary allegiance: to the audience, to the actors, to the playwright—or to some overarching idea that embraces all?"[3] These questions sum up the conscience of a director and are applicable to any theater situation. An RAS Theater should be willing to risk much in order to advance the frontiers of theater. It should continually question its directions, even if this threatens its own comfort and security. Every theatrical element can be used effectively. No new approach should be ruled out simply because it is new (conversely, *new* does not necessarily equal *good*). The ideal is a framework that includes both the new and strengths of the old. Whatever new forms a theater evolves, they will hardly eliminate the masterpieces of the past.

It is, of course, not enough to plan a paper season or say, "Since this is the play we should do to develop this theme, let's do it." Each play must be cast with precise concern for its obvious values or the values the director wishes to emphasize. If the first play to be chosen is, say, *Hamlet* (for the challenge of this classic is great and the eagerness of actors to undertake it always keen), it may not in fact be the first play produced, for several seasons of training and experience may be required before *Hamlet* is ready to be shown, before the company can bring new life to it. *Hamlet* might thus become a training work for the company and the period leading up to its production might include various kinds of special training and engagements in other, perhaps related, works. An RAS Theater should be able to plan such an arc of

[3] Robert Brustein, "Repertory Theater in the Doldrums," *The New Republic*, Nov. 18, 1972.

development leading to a goal and to realize the plan. For it is not merely by picking play titles that a repertory is developed, but by a scrupulous matching of roles with actors and other production values.

7

Art and Real Estate:
A Complex of Houses

NOT ONE OR TWO, but seven, eight, nine or perhaps eleven spaces will be needed by an RAS Theater. The repertory season might include some forty plays for the subscribers. Some plays will require large-capacity proscenium theaters, while others may have limited appeal and be ideally suited to small theaters or experimental spaces. The equation of artistic purpose and real estate is composed of several factors: the right play for the right theater, and vice versa, the location of the theater for the play and the audience. Establishing this equation is a matter of artistic projection and the results of research.

The complex of theater houses needed will represent all possible variants of seating capacity and audience-stage configuration and will probably be located in various areas of the city. Acquiring these spaces will follow guidelines formed on the basis of repertory and company needs. And the repertory and artistic point of view will also determine the design of the theaters.

A theater space is an area for playing for an audience. But it must also include space for rehearsal, manufacture of sets and costumes, plus storage space and parking facilities. The city will have to be combed for these spaces. Conditions will vary, but it is a safe bet that enough usable space can be uncovered for the first few years of production to obviate costly and chancy construction. When construction is appropriate, it should be clearly dictated by the artistic or working needs of the company.

The classic repertory suggested as the company's central concentration in the preceding chapter (and to be enlarged upon in the next) would require, for optimum effect, proscenium theaters, since most plays written after 1640 were conceived for production within the picture frame of the proscenium arch. Classic plays written earlier, and many modern plays, of course, can be presented proscenium style, or on an Elizabethan multilevel stage, on thrust, arena or other kinds of stages. Adjustable spaces are needed for contemporary plays which mix actors and audience. Theater designers have tried just about every configuration of audience to players. Some will work for one play but not for another. Not only are there varying theater configurations—rectangles, triangles, circles, squares, theaters with more than four walls, theaters with no walls and stage placements here and there, high and low—but there are also different characteristics to theaters. Two spaces with similar seating may have opposing personalities, the one intimate, the other grandiose. *King Lear* might be cramped in the first and spectacular in the second.

In order to accommodate large and small audiences for popular or unpopular plays, the RAS Theater should have at least one 2,200-seat theater and others ranging down to 150-seat studio spaces. A complex of nine houses might therefore include the following:

Theater	*Seating Capacity*	*Stage Configuration*
GROUP A		
1.	2,200	proscenium
2.	1,200	thrust stage
3.	750	proscenium

Theater	Seating Capacity	Stage Configuration
GROUP B		
4.	450	arena stage
5.	300	thrust stage
6.	300	proscenium
GROUP C		
7.	150	studio free space
8.	150	proscenium
9.	150	studio free space

The large houses would be for spectacles: dramas involving large casts, musicals, operettas, dance events. They could also house touring attractions. It is essential that the relationship between stage and audience achieve maximum intimacy. It is possible to get this in large houses, but rare. With poor acoustics (resulting from a badly designed hall), amplification can be used, but only when absolutely necessary, and then very discreetly. There are successful large theaters. Among them is the Academy of Music in Philadelphia, which holds 3,000 seats and has an intimate quality. The Stratford, Ontario, Shakespeare Festival Theater has nearly 2,000 seats and works well.

When box office is not the sole determinant, cast size and rehearsal expense need not dictate theater size. This is possible because the box office for all nine theaters would be centralized; planning of repertory and theater usage would take into account the aggregate seating and multiply that number times the average ticket price to arrive at an overall understanding of box-office realities. Therefore, artistic decisions of play assignment need not depend exclusively on theater size.

The RAS Theater needs large houses so that it will be able to run a popular production for large numbers of people over a given period of time. If the large theaters (those designated Group A in the table) have an intimate quality, they could even accommodate small-cast plays. And if a spectacle play that appealed only to a limited number of people were produced, it could be presented in a smaller, Group B house. Management, by having control over a number of theaters of varying sizes and configurations, would have the freedom to produce all the plays it feels need exposure and not only those the traffic will bear. Art should not be required to appeal instantaneously to the widest possible audience.

The mid-range theaters of Group B would be for those plays with considerable audience appeal. If appeal far exceeds expectation, a production could be moved into a larger house so long as the esthetics of the production were not unduly disturbed by the configuration of the second house. If audience appeal falls below expectations, the production might be moved into a smaller theater. It would be expected that the Group B theaters would be good for comedies, major revivals, small company plays and just about everything short of the spectacle—unless housed there for reasons of limited appeal.

The small Group C theaters would lend themselves well to any kind of limited-audience theater, especially contemporary dramas, experimental theater, children's theater and perhaps foreign or ethnic-minority theater. If a 150-seat house is the entire project—as, for instance, on Off Broadway—a failure will seem a disaster. But with a complex of theaters, and a large enough scale for the whole operation, radically different productions can be put on in the small theaters without much risk. Promising new plays can be tried out, worked on and, if there is artistic justification, perhaps moved from the small space into a larger theater during the season or later. This pattern has operated successfully in several theaters, notably the Royal Court in London and the New York Shakespeare Festival Public Theater. It is not unusual for a play of great shock value, deemed to have little appeal,

to become quite popular. Another example: Suppose a
director plans a classic production that is necessary for
the training of the company, but which will, he thinks,
have limited appeal. Production goes ahead, and while
the company is improving itself, lo, that play catches on
and people are being turned away from the door of the
small theater. Let us assume the schedule called for a
run of ten weeks. In order to accommodate audience
demand, the production could be switched from the 300-
seat house to one seating either 450 or 750.

The smaller spaces will accommodate limited audiences but their value to the theater is considerable in
developing new playwrights, new plays, experimenting
with form and content, and reaching children's audiences and foreign or ethnic minorities. In addition, the
Group C studio theaters can provide a platform for dissent with the RAS Theater itself. Suppose some company
members are in sharp disagreement with management
policy in an artistic area. The studio would be the sug-
gestion box in which the dissenters could try out their
ideas and present their point of view as an alternative to
management's. Community groups, too, might be invited
to use the studio spaces for artistic work or social pro-
test. There the anti-Establishment groups could present
their views. Controversy within theatrical communities is
very good for theater. It should be more than encouraged:
a place should be made for it.

Although artistic demands should govern the placement of repertory plays among the houses, the operation
of the largest houses must be given special attention, for
they will be key factors in the total economy of the box
office. Management will have to develop skilled and sensitive uses of the Group A houses for greatest overall artistic and economic benefits to the company. With several
large theaters on hand there would be less vying among
directors for control over this or that prestigious theater.

A play's running time must match audience needs. A Broadway hit show might run for a year in a 700-seat theater. Many people see it, but the long run bores the artistic life out of the cast. The RAS Theater could avoid debilitating long runs with an adroit use of theaters of varying sizes. With some plays a short run in a large house will reach a large audience, while other plays need long runs in smaller houses in order to build audiences. Some productions take considerably more than the usual four weeks of rehearsal. Peter Brook's historic production of *Marat/Sade* was in rehearsal for some eight months before it was ready to open. This kind of detailed preparation is essential to some productions and an RAS Theater would be able to provide for it. Once that state of readiness comes when only the audience can complete the work, the play must open. Since plays improve only up to a certain point in the run, a run should not continue past the moment of ensemble deterioration (a moment that arrives at different times with different plays and productions).

Care is needed in scheduling theater spaces in terms of reaching audiences. Suppose 20,000 subscribers are to be reached by one production. That play could be given ten performances in the 2,200-seat house, or it could play for fifty performances in the 450-seat theater. The rationale for assignment of play to theater, in sum, would be what was right esthetically, in terms of the quality and development of the play, and quantitatively, in terms of audience demand (projected and real). A poor judgment in assignment can be rectified if all the theaters are not in use and a production can be moved from one house to another. If it is not possible to switch houses, the rehearsals or run can be stopped and resumed later when the right house opens up.

It is to be assumed that enough theater spaces will be available for the RAS Theater to begin operation without having to build anew—and research would be required to substantiate this assumption. As the company members are being recruited, houses should be investigated. In 1927 there were some 600 legitimate theaters spotted around the country. In 1972 there were about 200. Not all of the missing 400 have been demolished—perhaps some can be salvaged. Any metropolitan area capable of supporting an RAS Theater will have theater spaces. These can include old movie houses, warehouses, lofts and such temporary structures as geodesic domes, outdoor amphitheaters and tents.

Renovation funds would be needed to put existing structures into shape. Planners should not shun this idea even though the refurbishing costs may appear large. Whatever is spent in buying and adapting will be trifling compared with current construction costs. And why spend millions on a theater complex that may fail to meet the needs of the company or the audience? Construction of a new home should be contemplated only when an RAS Theater is firmly rooted. Actually, if the company and audience are comfortable in renovated quarters, there may be no need to embark on such a costly venture, though the adventure and excitement afforded by creating new buildings cannot be ignored.

Whether a theater is new or a remodeled warehouse, it is a more complex structure to design and maintain than an office building. Scrupulous attention must be paid to detail. Because refurbishing and maintenance of structures can cause problems, a company would be well advised to design and construct properly from the start. This goes equally for remodeling and new construction.

It is surprising there has not been more renovation of old buildings for new theaters since there have been some marked successes. One example is that of the New York Shakespeare Festival, which spent only $2.6 million to renovate the old Astor Library into four excellent theaters, plus a film theater, a concert hall, other theater rooms and administrative space. The Astor Library, built in 1881, was bought for $575,000 and is a New York City landmark. It could not be duplicated for more than three times the amount spent on it. The theaters are highly usable and are among the most attractive in New York.

One of the worst theaters in New York, by most accounts, is the old Mecca Temple which serves as the home of the New York City Center for Music and Drama on West Fifty-fifth Street. This 2,800-seat barn has a poor configuration, a badly pitched balcony, a wide, shallow stage and gauche architectural appointments and decor. But despite its shortcomings, the theater has housed numerous distinguished companies which have played to large audiences at low ticket prices: the Moscow Art Theater, the Grand Kabuki of Japan, the New York City Opera and Ballet (before the New York State Theater was built at Lincoln Center), the D'Oyly Carte Gilbert & Sullivan opera presentations, even shows by the solo mime Marcel Marceau.

Many metropolitan areas have old theaters that can work. The search for them may turn up unsuspected possibilities. When the New York State Council was being organized in the early 1960s, I was asked to study theater spaces in New York State and I came up with an amazing list of houses with multiple capabilities. The most unlikely communities had halls for chamber music, theater, opera and musical comedy. Old vaudeville houses long boarded up were available and university and community theater structures were underused.

There may come the day when the RAS Theater, firmly established with its audience, can think of building. If the company is comfortable in renovated quarters and the audience response to those theaters is good, there may be no need to build. But if there is a need, careful plans should be made. In the spree of cultural center construction following the opening of Lincoln Center for the Performing Arts in 1962, many new theaters and concert halls have proved heavy financial responsibilities for communities and are dark for six months of the year —a waste of space and of maintenance costs. Some serve their resident companies well enough but fail to exert much influence on the community at large. For example, the John F. Kennedy Center in Washington, D.C., isolated far from the heart of the city on the shores of the Potomac River, has had scant beneficial effect on any of the impoverished neighborhoods in the city. And some cultural centers located in downtown areas of their cities neglect to allow room for the shops or restaurants that would attract the nonperforming arts public.

Most American cities can use the glamor and excitement of a cultural center, which provides a new focal point and occasions for festive beauty and bright lights. Civic buildings can lift the spirits as well as the tax base. Theaters, concert halls and opera houses are as important to a city's vitality and livability as museums, sports stadiums and parks. One trouble with the recent spurt of cultural center construction is that too many cities packaged all their culture into one monumental center whose structures are antiseptic. Urban renewal can be linked to performing arts centers, but more consideration must be given to the nonperforming arts public. An outstanding example of a close relationship between theater and community is Baltimore's Mechanic Theater, designed by John Johansen. This relatively small but assertive building is, in the words of one writer, "an integral part of the urban scene, the office and apartment skyscrapers, shops, restaurants, traffic and pedestrian plazas and walkways of Charles Center. There are shops in the buildings. There is nothing precious about it."[1]

[1] Wolf Von Eckart, *The New Republic,* Apr. 3, 1971.

Another well-known and admired theater, the Alley Theater in Houston, is like many other cultural buildings in that no attempt was made in its design to integrate its artistic function with the community. The Alley presents an imposing fortresslike visage to the street. Its founder, Nina Vance, worked with designer Ulrich Frazen on the building, which holds two theaters, one seating 800 in a fan-shaped auditorium, the other seating 300 in an arena setting. When the theater opened in 1968 there was general acclaim but some adverse criticism of the facade of the building. Miss Vance defended the fortress's blind towers and walls, which dominate the surrounding area.

What went into the building was more important to her than the building, but exteriors of buildings matter very much to those who see them every day. Design should take into account the environment and promote a sense of community. Shops and restaurants in such buildings are important, for they relate the whole building to a wider public. It has been seen time and again that office buildings that fail to include amenities such as retail shops and the like tend to depopulate neighborhoods. After office hours all the functions of the building stop and the area becomes deserted and inhospitable to nighttime traffic. The sense of humanity reflected in a cultural complex is increased by the activity of small shops. Lincoln Center planners failed to provide for such shopping facilities for the thousands of people in its West Side neighborhood and those who work in the center every day, although the senior architect, Wallace K. Harrison, and I both objected to the omission.

Though it is indeed imperative that the RAS Theater complex relate to the community in external features, the prime need is that it function well as a theater. Interior theater design has attained great sophistication since the 1940s and it is possible now to draw on a rich experi-

ence of theater architecture in planning new playing
spaces. The key consideration in theater design is that
one must be able to sit fifty or seventy feet away from
an actor, and yet hear him clearly.

Intimate thrust-stage theaters or arena-style configurations have had an enormous vogue in recent construction practice. Chief examples of these are the thrust
stages of the Guthrie Theater in Minneapolis and the
Vivian Beaumont Theater at Lincoln Center—by no
means the first such theaters, but among the best known.
The Arena Stage in Washington, D.C., has long espoused
productions in-the-round and its new theater is an excellent example of this approach to dramatic presentation.
The trend has also been toward intimate theaters, to avoid
amplification. Exceptions have been theaters built for
multiple purposes or to house touring attractions, where
large seating capacity dictated the design.

Gadgetry can strongly influence theater construction,
from the intricate modular plan of Herbert Blau and
Jules Fisher for the California Institute of the Arts
(a large cube whose walls and floors are composed of
four-foot-square panels, each of which was designed to
be raised hydraulically as much as ten feet) to the complexity of André Wogenscky's Mobile Theater in the Maison de Culture in Grenoble, France, which can revolve
stage and/or audience independently in either direction.

Theater construction places firm limitations on inter-
pretation of repertory, and to some extent on the repertory itself. The guiding principle should be to provide a
setting in which the world's dramatic literature can be
artistically interpreted. An artist of keen insight, of
course, sees possibilities in any space. Peter Brook is one
such theater original and he has posed some basic questions both in his work and in his book *The Empty Space.*
Approaching the ancient situation of performance with
new eyes, Brook asks the questions that should be con-

sidered by anyone newly designing a theater. "Now, the moment of performance, when it comes," he writes, "is reached through two passageways—the foyer and the stage door. Are these, in symbolic terms, links or are they to be seen as symbols of separation? If the stage is related to life, if the auditorium is related to life, then the openings must be free and open passageways must allow an easy transition from outside life to meeting place. But if the theater is essentially artificial, then the stage door reminds the actor that he is now entering a special place that demands costume, makeup, disguise, change of identity—and the audience also dresses up, so as to come out of the everyday world along a red carpet into a place of privilege. Both of these are true, and both must be carefully compared because they carry quite different possibilities with them and relate to quite different social circumstances. The only thing that all forms of theater have in common is the need for an audience."[2]

In this view the performing space is not as important as the ability of the actor to arrest the interest of the spectator, to "lower his defenses and then coax the spectator to an unexpected position or an awareness of a clash of opposing beliefs, of absolute contractions, then the audience becomes more active."[3] That interaction is the value of theater; the design of the space in which it takes place should be carefully thought out by those who will use it.

There was an opportunity for this kind of planning in the construction recently of England's National Theatre and the Royal Shakespeare Theater's Barbican Theatre, both in London. In these cases the artistic directors of the theaters collaborated with the designers in evolving optimal designs for existent companies with specific needs and styles. The National Theatre's planners in-

[2] Peter Brook, *The Empty Space*, New York, Atheneum, 1968, pp. 126–127.
[3] *Ibid.*, p. 127.

cluded Sir Laurence Olivier, Peter Brook, George Devine
and Sean Kenny, and the Barbican Theatre was brought
into being over a two-year period during which director
Peter Hall worked closely with the architects. The
National Theatre has its stage in the corner of the rec-
tangular space; the audience seats are steeply raked so
that playgoers are not too aware of their neighbors. Its
intimate size reduces possible acoustical problems. Peter
Hall's concept for the Barbican Theatre related to the
angle of vision that the normal actor covers as he stares
straight ahead—an angle of about 130 degrees. The
wedge-shaped auditorium that evolved from this concept
has a large, steeply raked bowl for the audience and is
designed to give the actor immediate connection with
them.

There is a wide divergence of configuration in English
theaters. The Nottingham Playhouse and the Yvonne
Arnaud Theatre at Guildford are nearly ideal horseshoe-
curve auditoria embracing wide stages with forward
thrusting circles which make for a sense of intimacy. But
the Chichester Theatre keeps its producers busy devising
ways of having the actors remain on the move so that
their faces and words are shared equally around the
arena-style space.

The universities are in the forefront of new theater
construction in America. Mistakes have been made, and
among the professional critics is the architect of the four-
theater complex at the State University of New York at
Purchase—Eric Larrabee Barnes. One such mistake, he
has said, was trying to "build flexibility into their formal
theater. They want a proscenium arch, a thrust stage, and
theater-in-the-round, all from the same facility. The result
is that none of these elements really works properly."[4]
A second mistake was making the proscenium theater of

---

[4] Eric Larrabee Barnes, "How to Avoid Over-Designing Space
for the Performing Arts" (interview), *American School and University*, Nov. 1972.

large seating capacity while the experimental theater had low capacity. Barnes suggested reversing priorities and building a gem of a formal proscenium theater and a barn of an experimental space. "Not only will the combination result in better theater," he said, "but will cost less."[5] This plan is especially proper for situations in which no single artistic policy is predominant, but in which the nature of theater work is constantly experimental. The concept does not apply to a major theater in which keen artistic minds have through a lifetime of work in theater come to decisions about theater sizes and configurations and their usages.

Outdoor spaces can also be utilized where climate permits. An outdoor theater was built on the edge of a ravine at Monterey Peninsula Junior College in California with permanent seating for 350 people plus additional seating on platforms and tree branches for another 800 or 1,000. This open-air theater cost less than $100,000.

In addition to the two ways of arriving at workable theater spaces already mentioned—(1) buying or leasing existing structures and renovating them and (2) constructing theaters anew—is a third approach, that of putting up semipermanent theater spaces. An example would be the Washington Square Theater, which was built to serve the embryonic Lincoln Center Repertory Theater until the Vivian Beaumont Theater was completed uptown. The downtown space was a low-cost installation and a highly usable one. Such a theater would be ideal for the RAS Theater during its formative years if it lacked a large enough theater to remodel.

Whatever method is used to put together the series of theater spaces needed by the RAS Theater, it will take the expertise of many specialists to arrive at a satisfactory solution to all problems. Dozens of experts, each look-

[5] *Ibid.*

ing at the needs of theater from his own view, will argue
over this or that decision at each step of the way in
forming the complex of theaters. The actor sees the theater from one perspective, the director from another; the
producer or manager sees it differently from the playwright. The combined thinking of many professionals is
essential. All conflicting points of view must be resolved
and presented to the architect, who will have his own
valid point of view. Esthetic and practical aspects must
be worked out in advance. And during construction itself
there may be constant modification. In building the
Children's Theater of Minneapolis as an adjunct to the
Institute of Art, the technical director of the theater
moved into the architects' offices and daily meetings were
held in which blueprints were red-penciled with changes
still possible to make on paper in advance of construction.

Because money can easily be misspent through wrong
or ill-advised theater construction, the theater should not
be built before the company has won its artistic spurs.
After its profile is known, the specific kind of plant it will
need can be built. Funds for construction would be more
readily available for an established entity than for an
unknown venture.

8

Making the Theater Work: The Playcasting Department

THE HUGE, INTRICATE OPERATION of an RAS Theater would be beyond the scope of any single individual, and although ultimate decisions on artistic policy might emanate from one person, only a team of professionals could carry out the day-to-day planning and functioning of the theater. Two teams would work on separate aspects of the theater under one manager. One team would be the Administrative Department, including the artistic director and the business managers who would handle all financial matters of the theater. The other team would help the artistic director conceptualize the seasons, plan the repertory calendar and then match plays to the right casts and schedule productions for the right theaters. This team would form the Playcasting Department, and in realizing the goal of the theater would be the most important unit.

In order to deal comprehensively with all the elements of casting a play, the Playcasting Department must include representatives from the theater's key units and must bring in specialists to work in the department. The department would therefore be divided into ten categories of membership: (1) the artistic director, (2) casting specialists, (3) playwrights, (4) directors, (5) designers, (6) actors, (7) technical directors, (8) the stage manager, (9) the house manager and (10) audience members.

The Playcasting Department would decide the individual working schedules of all personnel and the use of the various theater spaces. Scheduling personnel would depend on what plays were being mounted, their rehearsal and performance schedules and running periods. The working hours of the hundred actors, the directors, designers, technical staff and crews, visiting artists and others must all be worked out in some detail. And a work schedule must take into account salary arrangements, all union or other work rules, production demands and, in some cases, individual aptitudes. If an actor is assigned a major role in a production that has a heavy rehearsal and performance load, then a balance must be effected for that actor elsewhere in the season. Or, vice versa. All cannot be offered tailor-made schedules, but there should be a certain amount of matching of ability to work. In-house scheduling for the actors must also include time off from the company, either for medical or personal reasons or for professional engagements outside. Production department schedules must reflect production demands. A building crew might not be able to handle the construction demands of Plays A and B simultaneously, although they may be scheduled to open within a short period of each other; it might be necessary to schedule the construction of A far in advance, in a period of lighter construction activity. Capabilities of shops to handle demands of all the theater spaces is an important determinant of feasible limits.

The Playcasting Department would also have to match the play, its cast, the potential size of its audience and running time to an appropriate theater space. A spectacular play with a large cast may seem ideal for a large theater. But it may have a limited drawing power and would actually play to fuller houses in a smaller theater.

Conversely, an intimate play might be ideal for a smaller theater, but its leading actors could be so stellar as to attract huge numbers of people. It might, therefore, be more fitting to play it in the large house. Perhaps the theater wants to run a particular play for a month longer than usual because it is the kind of play whose performance by a company is improved by a longer run. That play could run in a smaller house where a slow build could increase audience size. Or, conversely, a play that can reach a large public quickly might be run for a short period in a large house.

1. *The Artistic Director*

The artistic director is the guide who sets the artistic goals for the Playcasting Department. Say the goal is a five-year survey of Shakespeare's Roman plays; or paired productions of classic plays and contemporary works based on the classics; or a Eugene O'Neill series; a season of contemporary plays on specific social issues; or an ethnic series. The artistic director would be expected to suggest particular plays, but that paper list is only the beginning. How is the paper season to be translated to exciting performances on stage? Which cast and production crew in which theater will bring a play to life? Casts must be as close to ideal as possible for each play.

The actors, director, designer and others must be able to express management's point of view with artistic distinction. If, for example, the theater wants to do O'Neill's *The Great God Brown*, the Playcasting Department would have to come up with the compatible production elements, and failing that should recommend postponement until those elements are available. Or it could suggest an alternative play to management, one that could be cast properly.

THE PLAYCASTING DEPARTMENT

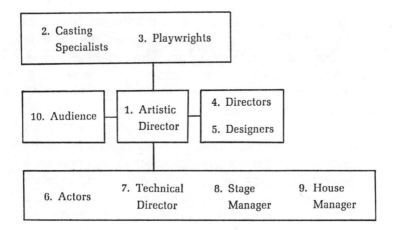

2. Casting Specialists	3. Playwrights

10. Audience	1. Artistic Director	4. Directors 5. Designers

6. Actors	7. Technical Director	8. Stage Manager	9. House Manager

The qualities of the artistic director are special. He must be an exemplary leader, an artist of experience, capacity and vision, capable of inspiring those working with him. He or she is rare. Finding the right person is one thing, getting others to agree that he is the one for the job may be another. It takes imagination and courage for organizations to appoint the right kind of leadership. Too often it is the merely nonabrasive personality that wins out over truly creative minds. Since a director is chosen by the board of directors (unless he is a founder of the theater in the first instance), it is necessary for the board to understand what is needed in this job. The artistic director must administer the theater, establish the artistic policy, set the tone and style of the theater, hire and fire and accept responsibility for the theater's successes and failures.

The artistic director's work will be realized through the Playcasting Department, which he will charge to carry out his policy and then work with to achieve his goals. The concept should be one of collaboration. This may be difficult to realize in practice, but must be an understood goal.

It is essential that the leader of the theater be a professional. Under that stipulation, however, the field is open. There is no rule to follow. Great managers have been directors, designers, playwrights, composers, theater administrators and actors. Luminous names among recent directors of theaters have been actor Sir Laurence Olivier, director Peter Hall, composer Richard Rodgers and designer Oliver Smith. An excellent description of the qualities needed for the artistic director's position were set down by Harold Clurman: "The director must be an organizer, a teacher, a politician, a psychic detective, a lay analyst, a technician, a creative being. Ideally, he should know literature (drama), acting, the psychology of the actor, the visual arts, music, history, and above all he must understand people. He must inspire confidence. All of which means he must be a 'great lover.' "[1]

In setting the overall artistic plan for the theater the artistic director must have and project a style. The leader sets the style, the tone, the pace, and most great artists have a single-minded concept which is the basis of their style. Style, essentially, is knowing not what is right but rather what is wrong, and eliminating it. The wrong note or accent is immediately offensive and obvious to the stylish artist. Maintaining style for him is not only telling others what to do, but also preventing them from doing the wrong thing. There are worlds of difference between a Balanchine ballet and a Martha Graham dance, but

[1] Harold Clurman, *On Directing*, New York, Macmillan, 1972, p. 14.

both share an uncompromising sense of style that instantly identifies them.

The style is the man. What the director must do is impress his sense of style on the company, sense the jarring elements and eliminate them, go from general concepts to specific realizations, break down abstract ideas and transmit their meanings to every department of the theater concerned. Great theater artists have in common an adeptness at communicating concepts. The director would begin by communicating his concepts to the Playcasting Department personnel.

No matter how lofty or practical a director's ideas are, they may be subject to attack, especially *before* they become visible in a production. How can they be defended when they exist only as abstractions? Until productions substantiate the style, the board of directors itself may attack the director's approach. (It is amazing how financial responsibility can convert the rankest amateur into an expert in theater.) One reason it is important to have a great theater artist at the head of the theater is to ward off such assaults.

There will also be attacks from professionals within and without the theater, and, of course, theater critics. These attackers can be defeating unless in the director's own mind his artistic concept is crystal clear. He could, after all, be wrong, if there is such a thing as right and wrong in style. An artist's work is not always accepted readily or, in some cases, ever. But leadership has to do with the strength with which one repels all criticism and refuses to allow confusion to creep in. The director's concept must be bigger than its parts, and it must be clear to all in the theater what the overall plan is. With policy well understood by staff, individuals can perform their tasks toward the common goal.

Whatever the director's state of mind it will be communicated to the staff. If he is confused, there will be arguments, bickering, intrigue, and finally, disaster.

If the director's style does not interest the audience, that ultimate critic, that style (or director) will have to be changed. Actors need applause. There must be an immediate and positive response for theater to live. Productions must attract ticket buyers. Presumably the director will not be working in a vacuum and he will be able to rely on an expert staff within the Playcasting Department. Any failures to communicate his ideas successfully to a supportive audience must quickly come to his attention and corrective measures be taken to keep the theater's work of interest and importance to the community.

Within the broad context of creator of style, the director should project his artistic goals in specific terms, such as by proposing thematic concepts for a season and the plays, or at least kinds of plays, that will further that goal. Consider what such a list might look like. Let us say that the artistic goals for one season included a series of Shakespeare plays, operetta and Broadway musicals, classic foreign plays, recent American plays, experimental and other contemporary plays, children's theater and perhaps puppetry or nontheater attractions. The plays would be proposed, matched with casts—if there are problems, perhaps replacements made for this or that play— and then assigned to the appropriate theater for a predicted number of performances per week and whatever length of run is justified by the demands of the play and audience.

If one of the goals of the director is to make the theater of service to all audiences—to involve as much of the community beyond the usual 3 percent of performing arts patrons—it may be necessary to provide a complete spectrum of theater to the public each week during the season. A visitor to the city during any week in, say,

October, January or May would have a wide choice. Listing the plays and numbers of performances in various-
size theaters will make this clear. In the following list
there is an attempt to cater to diverse tastes. Not every
theater would be used each week but there might be
matinees on some days at 10 A.M. or 2 P.M. and on
weekends there might be three shows a day in some
theaters, the last being the usual 8 P.M. curtain.

2. Casting Specialists

These professionals would ideally be former agents
who either worked independently or for major agencies
such as William Morris. Such agents have long figured
importantly in theaters as artists' representatives, sug-
gesting this or that actor or playwright, keeping names
before the producers. While the commercial agents and
agencies look after their own clients, the casting specialists in the RAS Theater would be expected to keep active
files on a wide range of actors, directors, designers and
other creative artists. These files would be the information pool that would serve the Playcasting Department
in its work. It would be expected that much casting could
be done within the company, while the roster of guest
artists would form the nucleus of star actors upon whom
the theater would depend for a considerable part of its
artistic lustre.

As has been said before, stars with heavy film or television or Broadway commitments have little available
time. If the artistic director wants a specific comic actor
to take a leading role in a Molière series, that actor
would have to be contacted more than a year ahead of
the theater's projected production time in order to find a
time period mutually acceptable for the engagement.

If the performer is interested, then the time spot must

Theater, No. seats & configuration	No. perfs. per week each	October	January	May
GROUP A				
1. 2,200 proscenium	7	Hamlet	Julius Caesar	Romeo and Juliet
	7	Pirates of Penzance (operetta)	Pal Joey (musical)	West Side Story (musical)
2. 1,200 thrust stage	6	Bourgeois Gentilhomme	Antigone	Dr. Faustus
	6	Long Day's Journey into Night	Devil's Disciple	The Way of the World*
3. 750 proscenium	6	Death of a Salesman	Servant of Two Masters	Ah, Wilderness!
GROUP B				
4. 450 arena	6	The Glass Menagerie	Under Milk Wood	Cox & Box / Trial by Jury (operetta)

5. 300 thrust stage	4	Zoo Story *Krapp's Last Tape*	*Slaveship*	*Bad Habits*
6. 300 proscenium	3	New Play	*The Way of the World*	New Play
GROUP C				
7. 150 workshop	1		New Writers	
8. 150 proscenium	4–8		Children's plays, local playwrights	
9. 150 workshop	2–6	New plays by foreign playwrights, poetry readings, puppetry, etc., film if related and supportive of theater		

* Indicates the possible moving up of a successful new play from a smaller theater to a larger one.

be worked out. If the star is unavailable for the period the theater has projected, then perhaps the theater should postpone the production. Or if the role can be filled by another actor, perhaps a special production can be considered for the period when the star is available, a play that the star wants to do and that would at the same time further the artistic goals of the company.

The process of casting might include numerous conversations with this or that actor before the final decision to go ahead with production is made. The schedule for production and the casting might be juggled for some time before the right package is assembled which represents the artistic director's concept of the Molière series. It is important that the choices be kept in flux until the right combination of play, actors and production personnel is reached. Then choices can be made and incorporated into the schedule.

In order for the casting specialists to keep in touch with the top professionals as well as to be aware of the promising new talents who might be emerging in legitimate theater, film or television, they would have to travel when important meetings of the Playcasting Department were not being held.

3. *Playwrights*

Other members of the Playcasting Department who would not be part of the production staff of the theater would be the resident playwrights. The expertise of these creative artists is necessary in making play selections. They would also give advice on the specific needs of adapting a play, or do the adapting. It would be expected that the playwrights would be working on their own plays and would from time to time have them produced by the theater.

4. *Directors*

The company's leading directors would make general suggestions both on repertory and casting. They would be expected to try to attract the best talents to productions they were directing, of course, and that might involve rejecting talents suggested by others. Directors should be able to give excellent advice on how much preparation time would be needed for a certain play and how it might best be utilized. This would affect the total scheduling of the season and personnel.

5. *Designers*

The designer is the span between conception of production and its realization. Designers work both for and with the directors, performers and crews that build the sets and rig the lighting. It is essential for the scheduling of the theaters and the manufacturing shops that the chief set and lighting designers participate in the selection and scheduling of the repertory through the Playcasting Department. They will be able to help answer such questions as: How complex will a production be in terms of set construction? How many productions of what dimensions can be designed and built in what period of time? What are the most recent ideas and innovations in set and lighting design and how might they influence the choice of plays, or the treatment of a play once it is chosen?

6. *Actors*

Company actors would join the Playcasting Department on a rotating basis, depending on their ability to function in the department and their own rehearsal and production schedules. Despite the basic concept of the productive utilization of actors, there will be times when personnel will be free of both rehearsal and production duties for as much as several weeks at a time. Since the actors are on payroll and are useful here, they could assist the casting specialists in talent scouting, or they could read new scripts or the like. The advice given by the actors, who would thus go in and out of the Playcasting Department, would add spice to the deliberations, frequently forcing the department to bring out projects which otherwise might not be considered—presumably ones close to the hearts of the actors themselves.

7, 8 and 9. *The Technical Staff*

Those deeply involved with the scheduling and maintenance of the theater facilities, of arranging the movement of groups of actors and of technical or maintenance personnel would be important voices in the Playcasting Department. These members would be the technical director, the stage manager and the house manager. These three department heads supervise all operations in the front and back of the house. The technical director oversees all lighting and the manipulation of the sets in rehearsals and performance. The stage manager is responsible for the conditions onstage and for scheduling the technical staff for rehearsals and performances. Anyone wanting to know when an auditorium would be free to use and whether it is safe, clean and properly lit, would ask the house manager.

All the craftsmen and support personnel who operate the theaters function under this triumvirate, which must marshall these forces and schedule their activities into the overall repertory plan. Rehearsal needs must be anticipated far in advance. In addition to regular rehearsals, extra rehearsals might be required and could be scheduled on off-days for production staff. With enough advance warning that such extra time might be needed, special schedules could be worked out. This eventuality should be considered during initial play selection and casting.

10. *Audience Members*

There are sources outside the company that should not be overlooked in the planning and they are to be found in the community itself—the metropolitan area and the subcommunities that comprise it. Since the theater will be wholly dependent for its support on audiences from that community, key members of the community should be functioning members of the Playcasting Department.

These nontheater professionals might come from several areas of speciality that could be of service to the theater. These include theater scholars, university professors and authors who could contribute ideas and expertise. Their wisdom and literary passions could help balance the performance-oriented theater. An Ibsen scholar, a specialist in nineteenth-century European drama, an expert on Japanese, Russian, Greek or other theater, or an American theaterologist would widen the conceptualizing power of the Playcasting Department and help further the artistic policy.

Sometimes in the community there are persons of great culture who are not theater specialists but whose wit and imagination should be actively sought. In addition, a theater critic might be a member of the Playcasting Department (although this affiliation could compromise his professional objectivity).

The interplay of the Playcasting Department with the inevitable pulls and pushes for this or that decision to satisfy this or that special case should promote an atmosphere of energetic excitement. The RAS Theater, with its polydepartmental Playcasting Department, should be able to respond quickly and properly to community desires as well as to the immediate and long-range needs of management. It would be flexible, able to respond to emergencies efficiently, e. g., if a planned-for production were suddenly in trouble because of an unforeseen problem— an actor is ill and irreplaceable—a substitute play might be offered. Postponement in commercial theater usually spells financial disaster since contractual arrangements dictate that schedules be stuck to as closely as possible. A cancellation of a performance for a sold-out house is extremely distasteful. When such problems arise in commercial theater, the necessary alterations are usually hastily improvised and damaging to the play. The organization of the RAS Theater on a subscription basis would avoid financial ruin in the event of a substitution, for it would be stipulated that the announced program for the season is subject to change.

Ultimately, every decision is a financial decision. Should the theater schedule *Coriolanus*, which requires seventy parts, or *Waiting for Godot*, which requires two? The number of personnel a play demands is an important economic factor, but it has to be weighed with other considerations. It may turn out that it is more economical to produce a play with a cast of seventy, if that play can draw large audiences, than to put on a two-character production that will appeal only to a small audience.

If the Playcasting Department does its work well, there should be few calamities, adroit adjustments in case of problems, satisfied subscribers and, most important of all, excitement on the stage, performance after performance. To translate the script to the stage with ideal cast, director, designers, technical staffs, adequate rehearsal time and conditions, appropriate performance schedules and theater spaces, without disregard for humane working conditions, will take much effort, much give and take, some luck. For even if everything works out smoothly and great excitement is generated, in the theater there will always be failures. Like successes, they too, must be absorbed.

9

The Theater Factory: Manufacture, Maintenance and Service

EVERYTHING IN A PRODUCTION that is not an actor has to be designed, made, bought or rented, handled and stored. When production sketches have been approved a production is ready to be assembled. Production involves three areas of professional skill: (1) the manufacture of effects, costumes, wigs, scenery and props in shops; (2) the handling of these effects for rehearsals and performances; and (3) the maintenance, repair, cartage and storage of them. Not only must all elements of the production be designed and brought into being onstage, but the theaters themselves must be maintained—stage and front of the house—and kept in good working condition for staff and audience use. Although no unique characteristics distinguish RAS shops from their counterparts elsewhere, the abundance of personnel required to man them, and the fact that all members will be part of the theater cooperative and have a voice in designing board policy warrants delineation of the task force they emphatically represent.

A clear division of labor should be followed but collaboration and cooperation are essential. Production staff execute designs, whether the effect is a trap door, a stone wall, lighting, silk slippers or false eyelashes. The builders and makers interlock with the designers, however, and all must constantly be aware of the needs of the performers. And their feelings as well! This is an emotional area and a difficult one in any theater. Performances can suffer when there are unresolved problems of design and production.

1. *Design*

The first step in manufacture is design. The designers work with the directors on the basic concept of a production. They often consider what will look good, make this or that effect. But equally important to the production is the adaptation of those concepts to the actors who will need to move with comfort within the production. The actor's comfort is a delicate thing and may be psychological as well as (or more than) physical. A designer may be preoccupied with the effect on the audience of set, costumes and lights, but if he neglects the actors, his designs may come to naught. For example, a circular staircase may be perfectly proportioned and have the right look from the spectators' viewpoint, but if using it makes the actor feel unsafe, foolish or just uncomfortable, something is wrong and must be put right. Not unexpectedly, many designers will castigate the actors for not properly using a set when it is their design that is at fault. And in a temperamental world designers can be tyrants too.

Two criteria must be met in any design: it must perform its esthetic function in terms of the play's values, and it must relate properly to the actors. The same holds true for costuming, but here there are some added fillips which designers could heed with good effect. The actor must not only be able to move well in the costume (and it must have the proper effect for that movement), but he should also feel appropriately dressed for his role. In a period play calling for elaborate Renaissance costumes it may appear an extravagance totally uncalled for to use extensive amounts of fine embroidery, good imitation jewelry, even costly undergarments which may be seen only in the dressing room. Such details may be invisible to the average playgoer, who only senses the effect of the materials. Second-rate materials might give the viewer the same effect, and save the company some money. This argument might be used by nonprofessionals, even board members. The only justification for extravagance is its effect on the performer. For a quality performance, not only should the costume or wig fit, but it should also make the actress really feel like, say, Elizabeth the Queen. The actor's feeling of well-being can easily be undermined by use of inferior-quality materials. The actors see and feel the velvet, embroidery; they appreciate the good tailoring. When there is enough care about an actor's performance to go beyond the simple needs of illusion in costuming, that caring can be translated into better performances.

Quality of costume is also its ability to survive many performances and cleanings. Some designers plan only for the opening-night effect and their costumes deteriorate rapidly during a run. In institutional theater, however, durability is important. A delicate gown that can be worn only once before it must be cleaned will be cleaned a number of times each week. Costumes must last and continue to look well.

The lighting designer also must consider the reactions of the actor to his effects. A darkened stage may have a certain dramatic effect but actors like to be seen. Near-obscurity may make them feel ludicrous and actually work against the desired dramatic effect.

It is the director's task to stimulate and maintain a healthy working ambience between designers and actors, for actors can be unreasonable and the creative work of top designers should not be inhibited because of the personal whim of this or that performer.

2. *Manufacture/Maintenance*

When it comes to building of sets and the like, the RAS Theater has two options: it can farm out the jobs or do them in its own shops. If a metropolitan area has existing shops where work can be done properly and economically, that may be a good solution. Most American theaters farm out their major construction work for they lack essential staff, shop space and equipment. The best situation for maximum control over production, however, is for the theater to handle all its own production, resorting to outside firms in extreme cases or emergencies.

The RAS Theater, in order to be able to handle the production demands for the projected repertory of forty plays in nine theaters, will have to recruit a large staff of skilled craftsmen. There is a difference between a master carpenter who builds a solid and heavy house and a master theater carpenter who builds a light and lasting set. The theater carpenter's trade is more specialized than his house-building brother's. A set must be strong and dependable but must also be easy to assemble and take apart, to store and maintain. Finding the craftsmen will take some searching. They need to have theater skills and also be able to work in an atmosphere that is often hypertense and emotional.

In addition, the theater will need electricians, painters, stagehands, costumers, each with separate functions and frequently different unions and work rules, despite the fact that manufacture and maintenance people often overlap in their functions.

All the shops are headed by a technical director, who, along with the scenic and lighting designer and the stage and house managers, works as a representative of the production staff in the Playcasting Department. The key specialists who work under the technical director in the manufacture and maintenance of productions are:

1. *Carpenters*, who build the sets and props during daytime working hours and who may in some cases handle them during the performance. One staff of carpenters could do both, but the more complex a production is in terms of scheduling, the more likely the two functions should be separate. The company, therefore, should contain two kinds of craftsmen: builders and handlers.

2. *Electricians*, who execute a lighting design, install all lights, electrical and sound equipment, create water effects onstage and operate all these during the performance. Like the carpenters, the electricians both originate the effect and execute it during performance. They set up the lighting plot for the performance and operate the lighting console during it. Electricians are also stagehands, and that title can include operators and repairmen of a complex electronic switchboard as well as a lamp operator who changes a gel or focuses a lamp for a lighting director. The spectrum of skilled workers ranges from elementary apprentice to master. The electricians must also be able to change over easily from one production to another. When there is only a short time between performances, say a matinee and an evening show, a number of electricians may be needed for smooth, efficient transition—which still gives them enough time for dinner!

3. *Wigmakers and dressmakers*, who, obviously, make wigs and costumes. A skilled wigmaker is a rarity in any city, so filling this post may pose problems. Minimum salaries for good wigmakers in New York reflect their scarcity, for they are paid on a level with musicians. Since it is not unusual to pay $100 per week over scale for a wigmaker, a good wigmaker can cost more than a cellist in the pit.

Good dressmakers are only slightly less scarce than wigmakers. These needle workers sew costumes and sometimes footwear. Costumes must fit, move with the actor, be sturdy enough to last several seasons under punishing conditions and be easily repairable. Creating a well-fitting bodice is one of the more difficult of theatrical arts.

4. *Scenic artists*, who paint the sets, backdrops, ground cloths, props and furniture. These members of the scenic shop follow basic production designs and work closely with the designers. Like the carpenters, scenic artists have specialized skills and must be above the general level of nontheater craftsmen since mixing and matching colors and following the color scheme of the designer takes skill and imagination. It can also be a quite gratifying profession.

5. *Stagehands*, who perform a variety of duties. Manufacturing stagehands are considered by many professionals to be the highest-caliber craftsmen in the theater profession. They frequently head production teams for Broadway companies where they operate or supervise production. There is a vast gulf between the skills of a "belly-lugger" stagehand—a man who carts and carries a piece from one place to another under supervision—and the skilled craftsman who has the ingenuity to rig and hang a complex, many-scened production, supervise its building, installation and operation.

Within the overlapping of manufacture and maintenance personnel there are sharp distinctions of subclassification. In a wardrobe department, for example, the cutters and tailors who make costumes rarely make small repairs or assist the actors in dressing. Other wardrobe personnel do this as well as maintain the costumes in storage in the theater and the warehouses.

Although construction duties are fairly straightforward, operation and maintenance work becomes a tangle of intricate distinctions under union rules. These distinctions in job descriptions and jurisdiction have been arrived at after years of bargaining between theaters and labor unions. Precedents have been established which were perhaps justified at one time under one set of conditions, but which, when taken as blanket rules for many theaters, defy logic. This problem will be discussed more fully in the chapter on the unions.

With some 100 individual jobs to fill, perhaps 50 of the craftsmen must be hand-picked—including the leadership in each department. It is essential that they be residents who can form long-term affiliations with the theater. Suppose an old production comes out of mothballs ten years after its last mounting? It would be well if the staff were familiar with it, for although the various pieces would be labeled, it would still be quite difficult to reassemble them. If the community cannot provide the skilled artisans required, they may have to be coaxed to move there. It would, however, be foolhardy to import semi-skilled or unskilled labor. If good annual salaries are offered, the theater should be able to attract skilled craftsmen and offer them challenging and rewarding jobs. In many cities in America it is impossible to get quality scenery construction and costumes by farming out the work. Where possible, the theater should combine some of its manufacture and storage needs with those of other local artistic organizations—opera or dance companies, for example. This sharing would increase the volume of work for the shops and avoid the peak-and-valley situations that cause detrimental patterns of overtime followed by layoffs, which makes it hard to keep skilled personnel.

In the complexity of its operation the RAS Theater may resemble a self-contained feudal estate, with its armies of craftsmen, artists and support groups. There must be constant forward motion and a spirit of humane goodwill and harmony, for success may depend as much on the balanced, harmonious working of all the contributing forces as on the dynamic performances of the artists on stages.

3. Service

As important as the upkeep of the productions is the maintenance of the theater. With many theater spaces to keep clean and safe for staff and audiences, this can be a heavy responsibility. Often union agreements cover the work of the carpenters and electricians in the offstage spaces, the lobbies, studios, dressing rooms, rehearsal facilities, skylights, cellars, storage areas in connection with signs, marquees, lamps, floodlights and other non-stage decorations. The personnel who maintain these spaces need not be as skilled as the stage crews. But upkeep of nonstage spaces can be a costly, painful portion of a budget and therefore quality workmen should be engaged even for this nonstage work.

There are also the service personnel who deal with the audience members from box office to seat. As members of the Subscription Department, they sell tickets and raise funds and process admittance to the theaters through subscription sales, publicity and promotion campaigns.

Another function of this department, which is in frequent contact with the audience and therefore must be capable of dealing with people, is to make appeals to the audience to donate funds without getting tickets in return. This is different from asking for a donation above the price of the ticket, and perhaps should be handled by a separate staff within the Subscription Department. There is a direct relationship between ticket buyers and donors, so if there are two staffs they must work closely together. The approaches differ but the lists overlap: one renders a ticket for a price, the other solicits funds with no ticket in return. Because the functions parallel each other, one person could do both, but the theater should have a supervisor for each aspect. In an RAS Theater there may be at least six persons working on ticket subscriptions and three more in fund raising.

After the ticket is bought the patron is in the House Manager's Department, which gives him a clean, safe, comfortable theater. The house manager's jurisdiction covers the cleaners, watchmen, engineers, security staff, checkroom attendants, switchboard operators, ticket takers and ushers. To organize and supervise such work forces he would need a staff of at least three assistants and a secretary. Although the number of employees in other departments might depend on the size of the theater operation, the house manager's staff would need to be large for it must work in shifts around the clock or from 8 A.M. to midnight.

One segment of the audience takes special handling: the press, the professionals for whom theatergoing is an occupation. They expect courteous, sometimes preferential treatment and generally demand information far beyond normal inquiries. A Press Department with at least three staff members is necessary to communicate the future plans of the theater to the press, to arrange for tickets and sometimes to provide office space for out-of-town critics.

Supplementary Performers

With a smoothly running theater company in a safe, clean, comfortable, well-hosted house, there will from time to time be a need for supplementary performers to the acting company. These personnel would be hired on a short-term basis, usually for special projects, and would include musicians, singers and dancers, acrobats, fire-eaters and other variety performers, children and supernumeraries, animals. For these categories supervisory personnel are needed in addition to the stage managers and their assistants. One would need, for example, conductors and assistant conductors for music, ballet captains or ballet mistresses and choreographers for dancers, choral directors and vocal coaches for singers, special personnel to handle "supers" and children and to coordinate the hiring and utilization of variety performers and animals. With a musical work, the musical director and the choreographer will become close associates with the director and may be on an equal level of authority.

Adjunct Groups

As the theater grows, adjunct groups may develop which relate to the management but are not a part of it. These, which should have a life of their own, would be auxiliary groups—"friends of the theater," women's groups, business groups and so on—which further the efforts of the Sales and Promotion Departments. They should be semiautonomous, not directly under the theater management. (In this volunteer area a young person may work so well that he looks to be a future member of the board.)

Auxiliaries do valuable work. The theater would be wise to empower one staff member to deal with these volunteers, a liaison to whom they can turn for ideas and guidance. Such guidance might suggest projects such as educational booklets, in-school programs or bringing children to the theater. They could publish a theater magazine or do other works that would call attention to the theater and attract new funding sources. They could serve as links between the theater and community groups. Leading artists could speak or perform at events for the auxiliary groups, and if cooperation is genuine, the groups may develop into important fund-raising bodies.

The general rule is: The less control over the volunteers, the better they will function. There is a danger that from time to time a volunteer group will get into areas the company would prefer it didn't, but by running itself the group develops pride, efficiency and productivity.

In addition to liaison with direct employees and "friends of the theater," all of whom work toward one goal, are those relationships with people tangential to the operation of the theater but who can affect the successful running of the organization. These might be union leaders and their lawyers, and the theater must, in order properly to deal with them, have its own lawyers, public accountants, insurance brokers and advisors. The theater management must also deal with outside agents hired by artists, playwrights and directors. These middlemen exert an enormous influence on the careers of their clients. If an agent is *for* you, he can benefit the company; if not, he can hurt it by guiding his clients elsewhere. This over-simplification obscures the fact that an agent's income is based on his client's and he therefore tends to guide the actor to the more lucrative opportunity. But, given a reasonable fee level, the artistic opportunities offered to the artist by the theater and the flexibility of performing with the company as worked out with the Playcasting Department, the agent should consider his client's well-being and seek to satisfy the artist's creative needs by guiding him to the theater for those periods when he would otherwise be inactive. Collaboration should bring satisfaction to artist, agent and theater—all vital to the profession.

10

The Economics of the Theater: I. Earned Income

NONPROFIT DOES NOT MEAN antiprofit. Like any institutionalized theater, an RAS Theater should be incorporated as a nonprofit entity so that it may be eligible for tax exemption under the law. In nonprofit organizations any excess of income over expenditure is turned back into operation and not paid out as dividends to investors. Nonprofit status implies that expenditures will always outrun income, and since this is the case in most performing arts organizations, it is a necessary form of protection for deficit-incurring arts ventures. It is safe to assume that in order to achieve its artistic goals, an RAS Theater will need to project deficit budgets. Two kinds of income will provide the funds for operation: earned income (from ticket sales and any other legitimate exploitation technique a theater can employ), and unearned income (from donations and subsidies). Although it is highly unlikely that an artistic theater will ever be able to subsist entirely on earned income, it is not impossible, for theater is the one performing art where fantastic profits can be turned on a property. Nonprofit theater must remember this and aim at earning as much of the total budget as possible, for two reasons: the economic base will be more secure, and donors are more willing to help an organization that is an effective earner, for it indicates the organization has found its audience.

All aspects of handling income and supervising expenditures will fall under the jurisdiction of the Finance Department. The head of this department and his staff must be professionals in their fields—accounting and business management. Planning the theater's budget will be the job of the artistic director. The budget, with its expected and planned-for deficit, will be executed jointly by the business manager (who sees that the budget is adhered to) and the comptroller (who oversees the relationship of the various projects of the theater to the total budget). This department will keep a history of the budget, monitor and solve problems of cash flow, report overages and shortages, issue warnings in case of impending financial crisis, and give guidance as to where money can be saved or earned.

The business manager is responsible for policy on expenditures to the artistic director. In small theaters the business manager *is* the Finance Department.

The Finance Department manages cash. While it is expected and desired that the comptroller issue warning signals about the ebb and flow of funds, it is for the artistic director to exercise judgment about how and where monies are to be spent. The comptroller must never be in the position of saying, "You are spending too much money and I am stopping you," nor must he be allowed to decide that rehearsal time is excessive or scenery too costly. By the same token, it is a foolish director who does not heed fiscal warnings and act upon them.

Planning the deficit is the business manager's job and his prediction of the gap between income and expenditure both defines the scope of the project in artistic terms and triggers the need to raise unearned income. Budgeting is guesswork that should improve as experience is gained with an organization. Unavoidable circumstances can deflect the keenest predictions from their mark, however. When that happens, and it is almost certain that sometime it will, the best course is to admit the error and redirect energies, redesign the productions, refurbish the theater, do whatever is necessary to correct the mistake efficiently and as economically as possible, and maintain the forward motion of the theater's work.

The theater's economic pillars of support will be the subscribers: those who buy tickets, thereby providing earned income for the theater, and those who give money over the ticket price or make outright donations, bequests or grants to the theater, thereby providing unearned income. The two forms are indispensable to the nonprofit theater, and in the chronology of setting up such an organization, unearned income will be needed first.

Before any tickets are sold the theater must be running smoothly, and that means it has to be fully funded. A company must be assembled, theaters leased and so on, all of which requires cash in advance. And before any of that, the feasibility studies upon which the theater is to be based must be conducted. The first advance money for such a study is called seed money, or sometimes front money (although a quantitative distinction exists, front money usually being the large sums needed to get a project moving and to ensure adequate cash flow prior to the opening of the theater).

Seed money is money for exploration—fact-finding missions to canvas one or more cities to set the parameters of the total operation. Seed money precedes the establishment of the organization and its incorporation as a nonprofit institution. The study resulting from this investment of seed money should be in hand before a board of directors is impaneled. The study should determine the overall capital requirements of the theater before the opening of its first season, and predict the additional amounts needed to enable the company to grow during its first three or four years and cover unexpected deficits. The study should find theater spaces in the community right for the theater and survey potential audiences for attendance and support possibilities. A seed grant of from $50,000 to $150,000 might lead to the creation of an organization with an annual budget in the millions. Before embarking on such a massive financial venture, an economic insurance policy is needed, and that is what the study is. It will allow for planning of growth and anticipation of deficits (which must be *planned for* and not discovered). Financial success is rare when deficits are not predicted with some accuracy.

Seed money can be obtained from individuals, corporations, foundations. In some cases federal and state agencies will provide it, but in general they are committed to established organizations and cannot bring new ones into being. In order to receive gifts from foundations a tax-exempt channel will have to be found or created. An existing tax-exempt organization might be willing to administer such funds: a university or arts group interested in the development of theater. For example, The Rockefeller Foundation in 1956 granted $50,000 in seed money to the Metropolitan Opera to conduct the studies that led to the establishment of Lincoln Center. The Metropolitan hired those who conducted the study to find a location, brought together likely partners for the venture, artistic and financial supporters and so on.

The seeker of seed money should first canvas all sources in the locale of potential interest for funds: wealthy art patrons, theater lovers, those who have made money in theater, film or television, local foundations, and state arts councils and any municipal organizations. If funds are not forthcoming from these sources, it would then be appropriate to contact the national foundations— Ford, Rockefeller, Mellon, the Rockefeller Brothers Fund and several others which have a history of work in the arts. However, if funds—or at least the possibility of funds—are not available from local sources, national foundations will probably be reluctant to help.

Budget Making

The RAS Theater, being a large business venture, must begin full-tilt. The planned economy of the theater sets the base upon which the structure must rest—to rise from it, or crumble. The dollar measure in its budget is not an indication of what is available, but of what is needed; it is a result of planning, not receiving. To set a financial boundary before preparing a budget is to limit the artistic achievement of the theater even before it begins.

Opera is perhaps the only field in which this large view of theater economics is easy to grasp. *Wozzeck*, for example, requires ten times as much rehearsal time as *La Bohème*. It has fifteen scenes calling for ten difficult scene changes. The preparation required can never be paid for by box-office receipts. Non-Wagnerian German operas don't appeal to large audiences; German works in English have even less appeal, and contemporary German works still less. So looked upon from the narrow economic point of view, there is only one conclusion: Don't do *Wozzeck*. But a grand opera company that does not perform *Wozzeck*—or a theater institution that fails to produce the theatrical equivalent of *Wozzeck*—is artistically deficient.

Budget making is deceptively easy. On paper, the budget can say whatever one wants it to. Marvelously flexible, it can show a surplus, if that is desired (by being too optimistic in predicting income). The budget must be made very carefully, gearing ticket prices and production projections to a planned deficit which the board of directors will be asked to cover through its own fund-raising efforts. A budget prepared for the board must be detailed, with expenditures broken down into categories as much as possible. Through it, the artistic director is trying to ensure at year's end that his income, including donations, will exceed his expenditures. And the board must agree to raise his projected deficit.

Remember that predictions are not facts. If the director overspends in one area, he must trim elsewhere, unless in the meantime income has increased. Easing up and tightening are both problems of communication. When it is time to economize, the company must be clear about what is expected. The budget may look authoritative, but it must be regarded only as educated guesswork. Like any guess, the budget should constantly be revised as information comes in. There is a danger of thinking that this piece of paper with its guesswork figures supercedes management, and for this reason perhaps it would be better to use the word *prediction* rather than *budget*, so that people would expect fallibility.

What matters is that more money comes in than goes out. In any budget the question is not how *much* was taken in or spent, but the difference between the two.

Nonprofit institution budgets contrast with profit-making budgets. A Broadway theater budget, for example, is simple in that there are fixed costs met by contract and variable costs depending on a percentage of the gross receipts. If a gross amounts to $50,000 at 100 percent capacity, one can predict covering the costs of performers and steady expenses on contract as well as the author's graduated percentage and plan a long way ahead at 50 or 60 percent capacity. Unexpected calamities occur for which insurance is needed. Since actors die, or get sick, it is necessary to have a reserve production very nearly ready as a substitute. The understudy system is another form of insurance.

Setting of ticket prices in either a commercial or a nonprofit theater is a prediction. What will the public pay? Sometimes with hit shows a prompt rise in price occurs because the prediction was too low, although it may have been accurate in terms of budget or cash flow. As more information comes in, the prediction—the budget—changes. Although raising prices is common, lowering them is rare. Psychologically it amounts to announcing defeat, and audiences resist defeated plays. Hence, the "twofer," the "two-for-the-price-of-one" ticket, or the student discount: the announced price remains constant but the number of discounted tickets increases.

A shift from seven to eight performances per week will change both the expenses and the income. The anticipated percentage of capacity is a great variable. The standard percentage is 65, but good management practice calls for an estimate on a play-by-play basis.

In predicting a budget for the operation of a major nonprofit theater it is necessary to estimate number of employees, set salary levels, gauge real estate and other expenses, and match the resultant figures with income. Let us consider first the expenditures.

Expenses will be based on figures including (1) salaries, (2) 20 percent of salary costs for fringe benefits and (3) 25 percent of the initial labor figure to cover rent, royalties and production. The concept calls for a roster of first-rate actors and staff, about 100 of each, or a total of 200. The rates of expenditure are different from one city to another in relation to a varying cost of living index. This index is known for every city, however, so an estimate can be made.

In order to guarantee attracting high-level talent management may have to set the minimum average salary for the company at $15,000.[1] Retaining the company of

[1] Two hundred jobs at an average salary per annum of $15,000 can be broken down in several ways. One way would be:

10 jobs @ $50,000
5 jobs @ $40,000

200 on salary for a fifty-two–week year will require $3 million annually. Add 20 percent for fringe benefits for a subtotal of $3.6 million for all labor-related items. This should represent from two-thirds to three-fourths of the total. By adding the remaining fraction (let us use one-fourth), which would include real estate and the like, a total of $4.5 million may be projected annually. All figures cited are to be viewed as guides that will significantly vary according to initial research findings on local economic conditions and the role of inflation.

Now, how to raise the total budget of $4.5 million per year which the budget predicts will be needed to operate the major theater? Assuming a fifty-two–week season, the theater would have to take in, through a variety of means, about $90,000 per week.

Budgeting for income and deficit becomes the next phase of operation. Earned income would include ticket sales for from 65 to 75 percent capacity. This amount may leave a deficit of considerable size—up to $500,000. The deficit can be attacked in budgeting in several ways: (1) organize with enough capital to cover the deficit each year for the first five years—$2.5 million if the deficit is $500,000 annually; (2) reduce salaries by 10 percent for the first five years; (3) expect contributions

---

5	jobs @	$35,000
5	jobs @	$30,000
5	jobs @	$20,000
10	jobs @	$17,500
40	jobs @	$15,000
20	jobs @	$12,500
40	jobs @	$10,000
60	jobs @	$ 7,500

total: 200 jobs

The first ten jobs could be arrived at in another way: five jobs at $50,000, plus ten part-time jobs at a rate of $10,000 per annum, which might be contracted at $2,000 per week for periods of thirteen weeks.

at 10 percent of ticket income; (4) raise supplementary
funds and seek major contributions.

A "manageable deficit" (a concept of nonprofit life) is
the sum one can reasonably assume will be raised. Some
considerations in figuring this deficit would be: Should
prices be raised? Should expenses be lowered? Should
expenses be increased slightly by employing a personality who, it is anticipated, will bring in substantially
more than what it cost to obtain him? Can volume or
attendance be increased by 100, 300, 500 seats? Can
the number of performances be increased? Should they?
What other uses of the theater will produce income?

In this last category several possibilities obtain: meetings, children's theater, chamber music, film series,
rental to a nonconflicting enterprise such as opera or
ballet, concessions (bars, restaurants, programs, soft
drinks, postcards, books, etc.), outside jobbing of construction shops.

The theater could also become a part of the local educational process, teaching Shakespeare by performing
plays. (The New York Shakespeare Festival Public Theater yearly gets support for educational performances.)
There could be two types: students coming to the theater,
or small groups of actors going into the schools. The latter
offers a valuable community service. Also, some private
schools are able and willing to buy subscriptions at regular prices. Electronic exploitation (to be considered in
more detail later), by making video tapes of productions
for showing on educational television stations at arrangements that favor the theater's economy, is another
possibility.

The nonprofit theater will be organized so that box
office will only account for from 75 to 90 percent of the
total income. This is the *major* source and how the box
office is handled is crucial to survival. If there are eight
performances per week over a fifty-two–week period, each

performance would have to cost about $11,000. If the hundred performers can give up to twenty performances per week in the various theater spaces, however, the per-performance cost is lowered to about $4,500. By increasing numbers of performances, costs drop; by decreasing them, costs rise. Box-office prices should not be scaled to guarantee whatever figure is needed. The theater's success will be measured largely in financial terms, but the significance of the box-office impact on the theater's economics must be limited from the outset. One assumes in the budget that donations will cover deficits. The number of tickets sold will be important as a gauge of the audience's involvement, but true success will be measured by the excess of *all* incoming funds over those spent or committed.

Ticket prices, therefore, must reflect a different goal of the theater. If that goal is to stimulate community involvement, tickets will have to be scaled at an average price close to the local movie ticket. This average—between $2 and $4 per ticket—will encourage students to attend frequently and takes into account the relatively small sums that the educational institutions and PTAs can be expected to pay.

Tickets must never be undervalued. They should not be given away. Theaters that have run experiments in low-price tickets versus giveaways discovered that although the same number of tickets was distributed in each fashion, the important difference was that people who paid came, while the holders of free tickets frequently did not.

Scaling ticket prices—setting prices for areas of seating based on desirability of that seat—is in some ways a lost art. The important questions in determining scaling are: What gross is desired? Why? A high top price gives a production a high value; a low bottom price lends a more democratic image. Whatever price is chosen, the question is: How many seats shall there be at each price? There are physical limitations to consider: the sides of the theater are not as desirable as the center and the front is usually thought better than the rear. But . . . is the rear center as good as the side front? So there are two possible kinds of scaling: center-to-side and front-to-rear. The prevailing theatrical scaling asks the same price for every seat in a given row, meaning the front-to-rear type is used.

Scaling involves multiplying the ticket price times the number of seats at each price. The policy of the RAS Theater should be to keep the prices a little low and expect the community to fill the gap in income by donations. It would be realistic to expect a 10 percent gap. If it is 10 percent or less, the board of directors is likely to pay little or no attention and the artistic director will be left alone to pursue his artistic purpose. At a 20 percent gap, the director will survive, though it is time to get cautious. If the gap widens to 40 percent, the artistic director will soon discover that every banker on the board suddenly has ideas on directing the repertory.

A policy must also be established regarding group sales and whether discounts will be offered. As with other considerations, scaling policy must refer to the overall concept of the theater. A theater may wish to strike a popular image by advertising its low-priced tickets.

Ticket pricing has been a subject of heated debate among commercial and nonprofit performing arts organizations. Critics of high Broadway and Off Broadway ticket prices have recommended lowering them. But the Eugene R. Black, Jr. study of New York theater in 1972 defended high ticket prices by showing that since the 1930s prices of tickets have only kept pace with the general cost of living. Costs for performance, however, have risen faster than the general price level.

In the commercial theater ticket prices often reflect real production costs. If that system were used in the RAS

Theater, tickets would be too expensive to attract wide audiences. Playwrights have even called on commercial theaters to lower their prices. When his play, *Indians*, was about to close, Arthur Kopit said that the $50 for tickets, dinner and baby-sitter burdened older audiences, as did the "theater ritual of dressing up." But "for young people, part of the groovy experience of going to a movie, standing on line, is being with your own kind." For three dollars one can "sit anywhere in a movie house. In the theater, he sits in the balcony and feels like a second-class citizen."[2]

The Bowen and Baumol study of the performing arts showed that:

"1. Lower prices do attract a younger clientele. In almost every case, for every art form, a rise in ticket prices produces a rise in median age of the audience group.

2. Students usually buy lower-priced tickets. In almost every case, for every art form, the proportion of students drops sharply as ticket prices rise.

3. Except in Great Britain, teachers usually purchase inexpensive tickets with the same degree of regularity shown by the students.

4. In the United States the audience proportion of persons in professional occupations falls and the proportion of managerial personnel rises with almost perfect regularity as ticket prices increase.

5. There is a perfect relationship between median family income and ticket prices: *the lower the family income, the less expensive the seat purchased.*"[3]

People do not flock to theaters with high-priced ticket policies unless a hit is playing. Only habitual theatergoers will pay a total of $20 for a pair of tickets, see a flop, but

[2] Alex Keneas, "Bad B. O. on Broadway," *Newsweek*, Dec. 22, 1969.

[3] Bowen and Baumol, op. cit., 282.

return to the theater again. This pattern of regularity is true also for film; seeing a poor film will not discourage the habitual cinemagoer. If the theater's goal is to attract and hold wide new audiences, then the occasional unsatisfactory experience, which is inevitable, must be made less unpleasant financially. If the theater here being discussed is to offer controversial plays-and-experimental theater performances, low prices will have to be maintained to lessen the sting of disappointment. Otherwise an unadventurous repertory will result. The cost must engender a sense of fair exchange, however, for what may be quite a few good experiences.

Returning to the budget, which called for a gross income of about $90,000 per week for the nine theaters, the following formula could be used. It is based on utilizing all nine theaters with the five largest houses playing six performances per week, the three smallest only three performances.

Weekly performances	Theater capacity	Weekly capacity
6	2,200	13,200
6	1,200	7,200
6	750	4,500
6	450	2,700
6	300	1,800
6	300	1,800
3	150	450
3	150	450
3	150	450
Totals: 45	5,650	32,550

At 65 percent capacity, the weekly total would be about 20,000 seats sold. If the average ticket price is $4.50, 20,000 ticket sales per week will produce the $90,000 needed to break even. (Many Broadway musicals gross more than $100,000 per week.) But if the theater's policy is to maintain low prices, the first part of the week's tickets might average $3.50, while the $4.50 average would obtain for weekends. The average ticket price would thus be lowered to $4.00, which would produce only $80,000 at the box office, resulting in a $10,000 deficit per week, or $500,000 for a year. (This amount is met and exceeded by several major nonprofit theaters and it should not frighten any major city.)

With ticket prices as low as a $4 average, the attendance figure of 65 percent of capacity may be too modest. If the number of performances per week were worked out differently, one could still arrive at the same box-office prediction. For example, the total performances per year of 300 (the result of multiplying six performances per week by fifty weeks) can be interpreted differently: One could play them out in forty weeks in the nine theaters, and not use all theaters concurrently. Adjusting the figures can be done in a variety of ways, and the two formulas suggested here can be further refined and improved upon. The essential point is that the major theater must sell one million tickets per year (over forty or fifty weeks, whatever) at an average cost of $4 to produce the called-for budget of $4.5 million with a planned deficit of $500,000.

In the metropolitan area that must produce one million paid admissions per year, perhaps 60,000 families would have to agree to attend the theater six times a year, assuming a family of three theatergoers. Or, 30,000 families who would come twelve times a year at prices ranging from $3.40 to about $5.50 per ticket. If those subscribers can be found or developed, an annual expenditure of $4.5 million can be planned for the company—a higher budget than that of most nonprofit theaters in the United States and most Broadway productions.

The audience is the single greatest financial strength of the theater. Box office derives income from sales of individual tickets and through subscriptions. Subscription, which may provide the needed cash advance for a season's operation, is a form of economic underpinning, akin to an endowment or repeated subsidy. In this context, community participation and pride should compensate for the relatively small percentage of tickets withheld for individual purchase. Subscriptions flourish when an exciting schedule elicits concern that tickets may not be available, supporting my conviction that the most invigorating artistic policy is the best business. When that happy day of 100 percent subscription arrives, it may be time to build another theater!

There are certain dangers in relying on subscription, just as there are in counting too heavily on grants and endowments! (Grant-making organizations can be whimsical and endowment in sufficient amounts to underwrite large deficits is hard to obtain.) A theater with a heavy subscription policy must give up a little freedom. Casts and plays cannot be changed indiscriminately. If a star is ill and the understudy is not qualified, it might be better to change the play so that an equivalent experience is provided. But since changing plays may interfere with subscription series, this must be handled carefully. The policy should be, in these cases, to try to give the audience the best. It will pay off subtly but directly in the excitement patrons will have on attending performances.

The advantages of subscription far outweigh the inconveniences. A subscriber makes a commitment, which eases the cash-flow problem between seasons. Subscription neutralizes the threat of bad weather to box office. The worst snowstorm of the season cannot materially affect a theater that is 90 percent subscribed on the night of the blizzard. The money is in even if the patrons are not. (A substitute performance should be provided at a later date for these people.) The stability gained through subscription allows for greater artistic experimentation because the last-minute box-office rush is not relied on for income. If performance standards are high, subscribers will buy in advance on trust, so long as the performer is the focal point of the theater. It is the reverse when the play or the playwright is the focal point.

Establishing subscription means setting up a number of different series of plays in the total repertory. For example, if the season offers forty productions, subscriptions could be arranged for a variety of those plays. Eight major plays plus two experimental plays; five and five; a reverse of the first; or any combination. Ten plays may be too much for some, so series of six should be offered also. For others, twenty may be too few!

Management must identify, analyze and predict the different audiences within the total audience, and what their frequency of attendance will be. Series "A" would aim at a majority which like classic plays; "B" combines the classic with the offbeat; "C" might aim at the 2,000 in the total audience who only want avant-garde and experimental plays.

Obtaining payment in advance for a series allows management to project the cost-income needs for each series with greater accuracy. If "A" is a series of classics, it will probably be more heavily subscribed. If subscriptions for a "C" series are low, that does not mean that management should change it to suit more average tastes or drop it altogether. To do so would violate the guiding principle: that the theater is an artistic venture in which both popular and unpopular theater are offered to a wide public. Management would simply have to work harder to pull the limping "C" series along with extra donations or subsidies to cover the income gap for that phase of the operation.

Scheduling of opening nights of the different series should give patrons a sense of excitement and glamor. Publicity and advertising play a part here. Although some subscribers are bound to feel they have been short-changed, management should attempt to schedule so that each separate audience is convinced they have got what they wanted from the theater. Scheduling new productions to open at the beginning of each subscription series is one way to impart excitement.

Among the ancillary earned-income projects already mentioned, the most important secondary area of earned income is the exploitation of a successful play through tours, film, television, and leasing rights. Speculating for profit with nonprofit funds would be foolhardy and reprehensible. But exploitation is a legitimate income-producing enterprise. It remains for the company to place its own restrictions on the limits of exploitation, for in the extreme this practice could harm the basic concept of the theater. There are numerous examples of nonprofit theaters which have speculated in exploitative ventures and made or lost money, among them the New York Shakespeare Festival Public Theater, which has made a regular and successful practice of transferring shows developed in its nonprofit theater to Broadway stages at Broadway prices. The APA-Phoenix toured some of its shows and made money, as did the Lincoln Center Repertory Theater. The Arena Stage developed Howard Sackler's *The Great White Hope*, and asked for 10 percent of the royalties. Mr. Sackler apparently offered 5 percent, which the Arena found unacceptable. It realized no return from the play it had spent $50,000 in developing!

In order to utilize fully the electronic media, a wing of the Playcasting Department should be organized to deal with exploitation of company productions through the media. The media wing would not only supervise and suggest material for translation, but would also raise funds for pilot television projects, film financing or cable-TV showing. Most television entrepreneurs are looking for properties. In a major theater, management should not wait until it is approached from without, but should exploit its properties as a matter of routine.

Funding from this source could be the most lucrative part of the theater's economy. Since this is so, the construction or renovation of theater space should take into account the possible need for television work.

There have been many more or less successful attempts to translate to film or television works from the stage. The most familiar, of course, is the complete remake of a Broadway play into a Hollywood musical in which only the outlines of the original play have been retained. But Sir Laurence Olivier's films of *Hamlet* and *Henry V* were high points of translation in which great fidelity to the original play was coupled with brilliant film technique.

When Richard Burton played in a Broadway production of *Hamlet*, it, too, was filmed, but the distinction of that translation was the near-genius with which it was marketed. The producer of the film pretended and advertised that he had possession of an unheard-of electronic process which he called "Electronovision." The actual technique involved changing the play slightly, using cameras in different locations and filming the play much as a live performance, presumably to capture Burton's spontaneity. As part of the production scheme, the producers announced that it was a special film of only limited exhibition capability. It could be seen only two days a week—in sharp contrast to the usual movie-house practice of showing films four times a day for several weeks. To the delight of the producers, the scheme worked and money was made.

A similar ploy was tried with the opera *La Bohème*, which was filmed on a studio stage in Munich, but which was touted as a film of a live performance at La Scala in Milan. In American musical films it is common practice to dub in singers' voices after shooting. The *Bohème* was a recording on film of an opera, not a movie in the sense of panoramic sweep. Nor was it quite an opera. Its producers also used the Burton *Hamlet* technique and sold reserved tickets for a limited showing of the "event."

The theater might consider several ways of using film and video, from simply recording a performance to remaking in the studio or on location. A distinguished production of a relatively static play—*No Exit*, or *The Glass Menagerie*, for example—could be filmed rather literally from the stage. A play featuring a certain kind of physical daring or virtuoso effort might be televised live so that the nowness of the event might be witnessed by all. The farewell performance of a great star, a comeback, the stage debut of an international celebrity or the premiere of an important new play also might warrant live telecast.

The theater could make a complete film or tape of a major play, and it could be distributed to each of the ninety educational television stations in the United States at a low cost per station. The investment could be recovered, some income acquired, and an invaluable recording of a production would be preserved. An archive of plays could be formed toward that day when telephone dial systems will enable a student in a distant city to dial the *King Lear* videotape, for example, from a central library and see it on his monitor.

If video cassettes and cable television are to be the heart of the pay-as-you-see television, as is predicted, this will probably open a golden door for the theater. The Sloan Commission report suggested that "There is only one stage remaining to [cable]: as a replacement for over-the-air television. It is not impossible that it will some day reach that stage."[4]

The British director Peter Hall has already planned for

[4] *On the Cable*, Report of the Sloan Commission on Cable Communications, New York, McGraw-Hill, 1971, p. 27.

the National Theatre Company of England to make its own films and videotapes. In this way actors could play in their own theaters instead of having to go to some central location. One question for America is: Where will the centers of cable production be? Will they remain in New York and Los Angeles, or will other cities compete? One would imagine that the city with a theater involved in media production would be in a competitive position.

Although the promise of electronic means of exploiting theater is considerable, early danger signs have appeared on the union fronts. And not just in America. After a meeting in Tashkent in the Soviet Union in October 1972 (in which representatives from thirty-five nations agreed on a three-page all-encompassing resolution calling for "international solidarity" on the part of the world's actors in fighting for better conditions now as well as in the future), the International Federation of Actors (FIA) issued a comprehensive warning to the film and television industries around the world, calling for caution in use of satellites and cable television for short-term commercial purposes, in uncontrolled use of recorded material and in use of imported material.

The three-page resolution said, "The underemployment of actors is generally caused by the insistence upon the arts of being financially profitable. For economic considerations, theatres are being closed and the drama content of television is being reduced. Added to this is the existing and increasing threat of unemployment caused by the reckless exploitation of performers through advancing technology. Communication satellites, television and videograms, if they are responsibly used, could be immensely beneficial to the spread of culture. Used for short-term commercial purposes, they will constitute a misuse of a miracle."

The countries agreed that actors' unions "must insist on achieving, as some of them already have, a quota system to prevent their national television and film from being swamped by imported material. It will also be necessary to have similar guarantee of a given amount of home-produced drama. By taking action in defense of their profession, the actors will also be defending their national culture. . . . The value of the actor's work will inevitably be diminished if he stands aloof from the people of whom he is a part and on whom he depends. At this time, actors throughout the world are seeking and accepting wider responsibilities by committing themselves to what they see are the needs of their communities."[5]

Obviously, any involvement of the RAS theater in the electronic media will call for special union agreements. This will be discussed more fully in Chapter 12.

[5] Quoted in *Variety*, Oct. 11, 1972. However, the "Theater in America" series of plays produced by regional theaters for the Public Broadcasting Service in 1973 was one indication that dramatic content on television could be boosted by using professional companies and that it was possible to attract grants for this kind of theater venture.

11

The Economics of the Theater: II. Unearned Income; Managing the Cash Flow

EARNED INCOME IS DEVELOPED through marketing a product. Unearned income derives from faith in that product. In order to take step one in organizing the RAS Theater, seed money must be brought in. Funders will be willing to donate on the basis of their faith in the project and the people behind it. The need for this kind of unearned income does not stop with the seed money for the first studies. Annually the harvest must close the expected gap between earned income and expenditures.

Whether an organization engenders faith in donors depends largely on its image. American society is willing to encourage and support potential, so the theater must project a reassuring sense of potential at the outset.

The world-wide economic crisis of the early 1970s provides an uneasy backdrop for this chapter. As the absolute costs of almost everything climbed, double-digit inflation eroded further the power of money. In the non-profit world, it was a time of belt-tightening and cries for help. Donor sources responded in several ways. Individuals continued to give substantial support, although there was a sign of diminished contributions. Foundations, caught with their own earnings dipping in phase with a

depressed stock market, tended toward conservative economic positions involving cutbacks of their annual dis-
persements. The largest of all foundations, the Ford
Foundation, having consciously overspent its earnings
for years, retrenched and halved its payouts, cutting back
from expenditures of about $200 million a year to about
$100 million. Its arts budget and staff were likewise
reduced, with grants expected to drop from the previous
level of between $15 million and $20 million annually
to between $4 million and $6 million. A similar drop in
general foundation giving had been noticed during the
first three years of the decade, even as the requirements
on foundations dictated by the 1969 Tax Reform Act
eased payouts from all foundations up to a mandatory
6 percent of assets by the beginning of 1975. This increase would seem to be of potential benefit to nonprofit
organizations, since it would mean that many of the
26,000 or so foundations would be markedly increasing
their giving. But the effects of the payout were still being
questioned by the foundation world and recommendations
were being made for revision of the 1969 law with specific reference to lowering the mandatory payout require-
ment of 6 percent.

Economic problems of arts organizations in general
were being widely noted and discussed on all levels. In
some instances, special groups and committees were
formed to look into the matter of support. It was generally agreed that foundations, corporations and governmental agencies could raise their donations to nonprofit
arts institutions, and that this was necessary for the
continued growth of the organizations which had so
proliferated in the 1960s.

The world picture in the early 1970s looked gloomy
indeed. But a long-range look at the ebb and flow of
economic crises in the world's history incline one to take
a more positive view. The problems of today frequently

lead to solutions for tomorrow and it is difficult to imagine an American society which will not place value on cultural activity as a prime quality of its life.

Fund raising is a major activity in the nonprofit world and the funds come in various forms. There are donations, which can be given by individuals or businesses, gifts from corporations either from their advertising budgets or from a corporate philanthropy, foundation grants and awards, and subsidies from tax-supported municipal, state and federal agencies.

The age of the wealthy donor has not passed. There are some individuals who are so wealthy there is almost no limit to how much they will give to an art, if it is their passion. Wealthy individuals and families have been the backbone of support of America's major symphony orchestras and its major opera and ballet companies. One problem for management to solve in establishing the major theater is overcoming the somewhat hereditary disinclination of the wealthy to support theater as well as the other performing arts. If this is successfully done, individuals can be of tremendous assistance to the theater. What is needed is a combination of extreme wealth plus a personal interest in the project.

In the nonprofit theater the bulk of the funding will come from subscribers in two forms: purchase of tickets and contributions above the ticket price. For example, suggested contributions from subscribers might be 20 percent of ticket price. A patron with a subscription for ten pairs of tickets might be asked to add 20 percent over the price of the subscription as a donation. If the subscription is for ten pairs of tickets at $10 a pair, the donation would be $20 over the cost of the subscription at $100. Patrons might be asked to give at least $1,000 a year above subscription price; corporations at least $2,500. It is important that top-level donors increase their giving as rapidly and at equivalent percentages to general giving. Thus, the economic backbone of the theater for both earned and unearned income is the subscriber.

Bequests form an important source of unearned income; they have accounted for from 8 to 10 percent of all giving to the philanthropic causes in America. The fund raisers should energetically seek bequests to build endowment funds.

Corporate support of arts organizations increased markedly in the 1960s, but these funds were regarded as minuscule by most professionals. The Business Committee on the Arts, an organization founded in the mid-1960s to create a climate among corporate leaders which would stimulate giving to arts institutions, estimated dramatic increases in contributions from corporations in both outright philanthropic gifts and funds channeled to arts organizations through corporate advertising budgets. This area, however, continues to offer more possibility than had been tapped by 1975, and the depressed economy seemed to have slowed down efforts to increase this source of support in the arts.

Corporate support for large ventures is well established in some areas; for example, the Metropolitan Opera in the 1960s annually received gifts from some 400 corporations. Some corporations give a set amount to organizations each year, rather than attempting to evaluate projects on merit and deal with complex proposals. The RAS Theater should appeal to all corporate boards in its locality in an attempt to secure funding.

If videotapes and TV cassettes originated by the theater are contemplated, the incentive to give might be strengthened when the corporation is told it would be entitled to a credit line on the final product. One minute of prime time, during the winter, on an average network television show can cost the sponsor of a color commercial about $80,000. One color-page ad in *Readers' Digest* can cost the advertiser about $56,000. It would obviously be worth a considerable sum to the corporation to be associated for an indefinite period with a leading theater. A soap company may want to get away from its image as sponsor of "soap operas." Sponsorship of the theater would buy prestige and risk very little, although it is possible the corporation will find itself sponsoring an institution that expresses anticorporate or other controversial biases. The corporate donor should be advised to consider the content of a broad range of the repertory rather than an isolated play which might seem unpalatable.

Since the passing of the 1969 Tax Reform Act, the foundation world has changed. According to one source, "Eighty-four percent of the [2,497 foundations] were set up after 1940, but even with incomplete data for the decade of the 1970s, it is evident that the growth curve is declining markedly."[1]

Of the national foundations, Ford and Rockefeller have played important roles in the development of theaters. Ford, which has considerably more dispersible funds each year than Rockefeller, has made the broadest impact on nonprofit theater in America through its funding of regional theaters all over the country. The Arena, Alley, ACT, Guthrie—there is almost no important regional theater that has not been helped by Ford Foundation contributions. Programs have included training and assistance for every phase of theater work.

[1] *The Foundation Directory*, Edition 5, 1975, New York, Columbia University Press. The Foundation Center in New York is a clearing house of information on all foundation activity. It publishes annual reports on foundation gifts in units of $5,000 and up, and is an important reference for fund-raisers to ascertain possible avenues to pursue. Another important source of information is the Council on Foundations, Inc., supported by some 735 grant-making United States foundations, with offices in New York City.

The Rockefeller Foundation, with its relatively small amounts for the arts each year, has concentrated on helping the playwright, and has supported, in addition to individual playwrights, some theaters which help the new playwright, such as the New York Shakespeare Festival Public Theater, Cafe LaMama, the Eugene O'Neill Memorial Theater Center (which it helped establish) and the Office of Advanced Drama Research at the University of Minnesota (another Rockefeller Foundation offspring).

Foundation contributions have had an immense impact on the performing arts in America. One could scarcely imagine their growth and progress in the 1960s without the few foundations that gave for projects. A rule of thumb with foundations, however, is not to expect a relationship to last forever. Foundations are responsible to the board chairman and the president, so the foundation's course will change from time to time. A ten-year relationship with a major foundation is quite good. Five years is not unusual, although two or three years of funding is more common. Foundations are besieged with applications for funds, and regardless of how large their endowments seem to the outsider, the expendable funds *are* limited. Priorities are usually set and observed. The term "guideline" means the limits of a foundation's interest, although it may seem to applicants a convenient way to frame declination letters. In approaching a foundation it is wise to know what its guidelines really are. These can be determined by reading annual reports and presidential statements, and by examining in those annual reports the grants to organizations for specific purposes over a year's time.

The best guide to approaching a foundation was summed up by Thomas R. Buckman, president of The Foundation Center, in his Introduction to Edition 5 of *The Foundation Directory*, and I quote his four rules for grant application:

"1. Do your homework. Know the foundation's areas of interest and objectives and its potential for support.

2. Submit only those proposals which fall within the foundation's areas of interest and within its means.

3. Clear with the foundation before you prepare and submit lengthy proposals.

4. If you receive a grant, make regular evaluation and progress reports with a sufficiently detailed accounting of expenditures of foundation funds."[2]

Because foundations will not be loyal givers for long, it is best to approach them with project proposals for their specific involvement over a short spread of years. Foundations could put up seed money for feasibility studies and then be asked to contribute to starting costs over a period. Since a foundation is usually leery of being made the big brother in financial arrangements, it would be well to ask for not more than one-third of a total budget from any single foundation. Indeed, the more sources, the broader the base of support, and the more secure an organization will be. As with the stock market, in diversification there is strength.

If foundations are too inconstant to be considered permanent marriage partners, they might be wooable for new affairs. If an organization's management has done what it said it would with past grant funds—and has done it well—a foundation might be willing to consider continued interest. Such new projects could include a liaison with a university, a new building, developing other major projects, commissioning new plays.

One definition of subsidy is, funds derived from tax sources to offset operational deficits or to guarantee continuity of operation. When the federal government provides subsidy funds to transportation industries, for ex-

[2] *Ibid.*

ample, it is usually to ensure the continuing service of a company by making up a deficit occurring in the budget. Although subsidies exist at federal, state and municipal levels in many forms, such tax monies in support of arts activities are more recent. And, in general, these sources of funding avoid the traditional concept of subsidy.

For example, the National Endowment for the Arts clearly states that it does not "give 'general support' grants."[3] This policy, albeit firmly entrenched in the traditions of the Endowment, is nevertheless at variance with other attitudes toward subsidy in other areas of federal interest, and the question should be asked, Why should arts organizations be treated any differently from organizations receiving subsidy in industry, education, farming or other areas? Similar guidelines obtain at various state arts councils, including the inability in general to fund organizations less than a year or two old. And tax-source funding agencies tend to stress demographic equity in disbursement of funds which can be reflected in a per capita system. For example, the New York State Council on the Arts, under its mandate to distribute its funds on a per capita basis, may fund an organization in Manhattan to perform in Queens, and use the audience figures of Queens residents in attendance to justify the funds having gone to the Manhattan organization. This enables the top quality organizations to receive the help they may require and at the same

[3] National Endowment for the Arts, Guide to Programs, July 1974, National Endowment for the Arts, Washington, D.C. This is one of four areas generally not funded by the Endowment. The other three being 1) "grants for deficit funding, capital improvements or construction, purchase of permanent equipment or real property"; 2) "organizational grants (which) provide more than half of the total cost of the project"; and 3) "tuition assistance for college and university study in the United States or abroad."

time makes their services available to large segments of the public not normally reached.

There has been a chronic fear that if government supports the arts, it will attempt to dictate policy in a heavy-handed manner, especially since Congress or state legislatures must vote annual funds. Some remember the congressional investigation of the WPA in the 1930s and the summary cutting off of funds to the highly successful Federal Theater—a milestone in American theater. One congressional investigator actually asked Hallie Flanagan Davis, the head of the WPA Theater project, if the seventeenth-century English playwright Christopher Marlowe (whose *Dr. Faustus* had been given a controversial production by The Mercury Theater Company of Orson Welles and John Houseman) was a Communist!

City governments are newcomers to performing arts subsidy although they have supported other cultural institutions such as libraries and art museums. Expecting cities with calamitous urban problems to give more attention to the arts may be unrealistic, but New York City has been willing to support the New York Shakespeare Festival, the Brooklyn Academy of Music and other organizations, and other cities may be willing to give similar support. The argument that should be put forth is that cultural institutions are an important asset to a city whether or not large numbers of the populace frequent them. The interdependency of cultural institutions and businesses such as hotels and restaurants has firmly been established. These and other tourist businesses suffer when cultural organizations do poorly. And, conversely, a thriving theater can lift a neighborhood. The example of the Trinity Square Playhouse in Providence, Rhode Island, is a good one. This theater acquired and renovated an old vaudeville and movie house—the Majestic Theater—in downtown Providence and began producing its plays there. Shortly after its opening in December 1973 a

defunct restaurant nearby was resuscitated and a new
liveliness was generated in what had been a deteriorat-
ing section of the city. As business increases in such an
area, and more people frequent it, land values are sure
to climb and city tax receipts rise. Any councilman capable of seeing this relationship between art and tax
revenues would be likely to favor direct municipal support of an art organization through purchase of its buildings (on a dollar-a-year rental basis) or by direct subsidy
of its programs.

At a time when most Americans interested in the economics of arts organizations were looking with increased
hopes at tax sources for funding, European leaders in
countries long noted for subsidized theater, music and
dance were beginning to wonder how to increase their
private sources of funding! By 1975 it was apparent that
the concern over the economic problems of arts institutions in the United States was becoming more and more
widespread, and that citizens' groups and many agencies
were working in a cooperative spirit to find solutions.
These signs are good, and point to a more secure relationship among nonprofit organizations, the private foundations, corporations and governmental support agencies.

No matter how generous government or foundation
support may be, it is no substitute for local audience
support, and success in winning the former should cause
no letup in vigorous community fund-raising efforts.
For example, if a total of $6 million is needed by a thea-
ter, and government agencies or foundations have indicated a possibility of providing $1 million, the fund rais-
ers should still try to raise the total $6 million from other
sources. Then if the $1 million actually materializes, it
will be an overage providing an extra margin of economic security.

Once the funds for the project's launching have been
amassed and management begins to operate with its

board of directors, fund raising becomes a normal and relentless part of the day's work. The fund raisers on the staff will keep busy making new contacts with potential donors and keeping the lines of friendly communication open with old ones. The artistic director may find himself called upon to make an occasional appearance for fund-raising—at a society dinner or a meeting of corporate or foundation officers—for his glamor, flamboyance, dash or elegant style may accomplish more than the best staff. But this use of an artistic director's time is largely inappropriate and should be minimized.

A poor management, trusting to luck, may allow the income-expenditure gap to grow too wide. It has already been said that an unplanned deficit of 10 percent will earn the director high marks from his board. If it grows, the board becomes nervous. A mid-season or end-of-season financial panic will actually frighten away donors. The board should not have to instruct the director how to manage, but should either approve his budgetary predictions and techniques or get a new director.

Crises do develop, some genuine, some only fund-raising techniques. A classic example of expert handling of a true crisis in unearned income is shown by a letter of appeal for funds for the APA-Phoenix Theater of October 1968. Addressed "Dear Friend," it read, in part, "We have a crisis . . . and strangely enough it comes at a time of great life and hope in our company." There were 19,000 subscribers for what was called "the best repertory company in America," a season of forty-two weeks, low prices, school programs, free theater in the summer. But government support was relied upon: "We took for granted the continuing contribution of the National Endowment. This year the Congress in Washington slashed their appropriations, reasoning that the arts have no claim for support when there is a war on and when America has problems in every urban area." The resultant unplanned deficit, therefore, was $250,000, or 20 percent of the theater's needs. The theater turned to the city for that sum.

The theater actually raised its money by touring its successful production of George Kelly's *The Show-Off*, which featured Helen Hayes. T. Edward Hambleton, founder of both the Phoenix and the APA and later of the joint APA-Phoenix Theater, later said the tour "has given us a new lease on life, some cash to go with it, and a strong belief that, with the help of our audience and the New York community, we can replace the National Endowment's lost $250,000 by Christmas [1968]." Unfortunately the APA-Phoenix did not survive the 1969 season.

One measure of success is the ability of a theater to close a wide income-expenditure gap. The 20 percent gap the Phoenix suffered was too large ultimately to be borne, and the company's work failed to engender the fervent support needed to sustain that level of unearned income. Though it ultimately failed, the theater's approach illustrates the classic clarion call for unearned income: "We are an artistic success, not a failure; but we need money." Excitement on stage produces check writing at home.

Another example of this kind of pleading from success came from the executive director of the New York City Center, Norman Singer, who, in reporting the City Center's first failure in its twenty-nine–year history to cover operating costs by revenues and contributions, said, "We find the more we do, the more money we are able to raise." The unplanned deficit for the 1971–1972 season amounted to $1.3 million and was carried into the next season. The City Center's fund-raising techniques included an important auxiliary association, the Friends of City Center, which had a membership of 8,000 and had raised $750,000. The Friends' efforts included running thrift shops, giving parties, holding raffles.

The Minnesota Theater Company (the Guthrie Theater) experienced grave economic problems in 1969 which were partially solved by a successful fund-raising campaign in 1971 that offered the unique *non*bargain of five tickets for the price of six. Subscriptions had declined steadily from a high in 1963 of 21,295 to a low in 1970 of only 9,622. This would spell disaster for any theater, and almost did for the Guthrie. The usual techniques of offering discounts to subscribers failed to bolster the sagging lists. By 1970 the percentage of gross revenue was running 15 percent below the percentage of audience capacity. That year, Michael Langham was made artistic director and a consulting firm brought in. It was the consultants who thought of and developed a five-for-the-price-of-six concept that succeeded.

After some initial shock and rejection, the subscribers rallied. In 1971, with no increase in ticket prices but with subscribers paying for a bogus "sixth ticket," income per subscriber rose by 40 percent. The gap between percent of capacity and percent of possible gross ticket income had been halved. The "sixth-ticket" gifts brought in a total of $20,000 and there were 2,665 small gifts to the theater, nearly twenty-five times more than in the preceding year.

Donors have shown they will respond to specific needs in other art forms as well. The Minnesota Orchestra, for example, matched a 1966 challenge grant of $2 million from the Ford Foundation, which stipulated that the orchestra raise $4 million. Its optimistic board set the goal at $10 million instead and by 1970 had exceeded that considerably. The success of this fund raising was based on artistic leadership. Kenneth Dayton, chairman of the fund drive, said the success of that campaign was the result of the board's determination to make the orchestra one of the world's greatest, and the community came to its support. This kind of thinking has yet to be widely applied to theater.

It is not easy to raise money for housekeeping. Amyas

Ames, president of Lincoln Center, Inc., said in 1969 that he foresaw difficulties in finding the money to meet the administrative and housekeeping costs because these were not regarded as "exciting projects." Once these costs were met, however, he felt certain that money would be forthcoming for the more attractive artistic undertakings.

The major need of any organization is for "housekeeping" costs or maintenance. It has been said that the maintenance or "hidden money" costs can be substantial and ruinous if not anticipated and covered. It makes sense to minimize the amount of these costs whenever possible. Occupants of new buildings must spend substantial amounts on keeping windows clean and the building functioning safely and properly. One way of cutting down on these costs is to share central costs and facilities with other organizations. Several organizations can share one source of heat, air-conditioning and so forth. This is a key concept of the Lincoln Center affiliation, where shared costs include maintenance of the fountains, as well as the essential needs—heat and climate control.

Another way to meet housekeeping costs is through municipal ownership of the physical plant. By getting New York City to buy and pay for the renovations of the old Astor Library, Joseph Papp solved the problems of restoration and future maintenance of the building. An emergency appeal in June 1970 to guarantee the summer season that year resulted in the formation of the Committee to Save the New York Shakespeare Festival in December 1970 under the chairmanship of Roger L. Stevens. The committee served as a public advocate, not a fund raiser, but it did help convince City Hall to purchase the Public Theater, which greatly reduced the costs of operating that large operation. Another way to cut down on housekeeping costs is through affiliations with colleges or universities, which can offer rent-free facilities and supply maintenance costs as well.

What does one do when the theater actually makes money? This can happen and frequently does in non-profit organizations when box office realizes the amount originally predicted, unearned income exceeds original predictions, or costs are less than anticipated. Suppose a theater advertised that it came out ahead? Giving would probably fall off and the following year could be a financial disaster. To maintain support the theater must project a constant sense of financial need. To do this there are several ways of dealing with overages.

One arrangement is to put the excess donated funds not designated for specific purposes into an endowment fund, thereby subtracting from the total income enough money to show a deficit at season's end. Actually it is not a bad idea to begin to build endowment, for such funds have two highly advantageous characteristics: (1) they are an automatic cash reserve in time of need and (2) the interest earned from endowment is the purest form of unearned income.

One theater that dealt well with an overage was the American Conservatory Theater of San Francisco. Its management realized that an unearned income overage is not a profit, so it did not allow confusion to arise in the minds of the donors that the theater made money. The ACT ended its 1971–1972 season with a surplus of about $120,000. This was produced by an earned income of $760,000 and donations of about $612,000, which produced a total of $1,372,000. Expenditures for the season came to only $1,252,000. In its public accounting the overage was *not* treated by ACT as a surplus of 10 percent; rather it was placed in a specially created category in the budget summary called "Reserved for Deficit Reduction or Contingency." This legal way of treating a surplus recognizes the lean-year–fat-year syndrome, and

is practiced by most sophisticated arts organizations lucky
enough to experience overages. ACT could as well have
designated the funds for endowment.

The need for endowment funds has been long recognized. The Ford Foundation's $80.2 million program of
challenge grants to symphony orchestras was an enormous effort to establish or increase endowments for
musical organizations. Smaller organizations, too, recognize this need, and in its annual report for the 1971–
1972 season the Chamber Music Society of Lincoln Center
announced the beginning of a drive for endowment funds
for the then three-year-old society. The society stated it
had "earned $114,404 from ticket sales in New York and
$13,673 from Washington. Of the total expense of
$313,167, $128,077 were met through box office receipts,
$40,396 from investment income, and the remaining
deficit through private gifts and foundation grants. . . .
The Society has embarked on an endowment campaign
with a goal of $5,000, 000. We have already received gifts
and pledges totalling $1,042,250 and are eager to reach
our goal as soon as possible by appealing to those with a
special interest in the Society's program."[4]

The society then offered the opportunity for donors to
give to endow the commissioning program, the educational program, the resident artists' chairs, the guest artist program, and the privilege of naming six boxes, the
artists' dressing rooms and various seats in Alice Tully
Hall. This allowed donors to earmark funds and thereby
play a decision-making role, in contrast to the anonymity
of most endowment giving.

The hopeful answer of endowment was treated in the
January 1971 issue of *Financing the Arts*.[5] It declared that

[4] *Annual Report*, Chamber Music Society of Lincoln Center,
1972.
[5] A publication of the C. W. Shaver & Company, Inc., New
York.

until the Ford Foundation had offered the unprecedented $80.2 million to the orchestras in the mid-1960s, "the rich potential for new or increased endowment income for the performing arts was largely unexplored. The Ford Foundation sought to consolidate the nation's rich orchestral resources, advance the quality of orchestras by enabling more musicians to devote their major energies to orchestral performance, attract more young people of talent to professional careers in orchestras by raising the income and prestige of symphony musicians, and extended the range of orchestra services to larger and more diversified audiences."

The Shaver newsletter points to several concepts that are needed in the successful raising of endowment: "Years of counseling arts organizations, colleges, universities and other philanthropic institutions have resulted in the formation of 'Shaver's Laws,' [such as] 'Success in raising endowment funds can be directly related to the ability to interpret the use of endowment income in the solution of problems. *Endowment is dynamic, not static*' [and] 'Success in raising endowment funds will be directly related to success in the management of endowment funds.' "

In mounting successful endowment drives to match the Ford Foundation's challenge grants, it was essential that orchestra managements show donors how endowment monies would be used. One way of tagging such funds was to create programs for "endowed chairs"—a technique used later by the Chamber Music Society of Lincoln Center. So much endowment money would pay the salary of the first chair player in each section of the orchestra. In its fund raising of more than $10 million the Minnesota Orchestra earmarked about $5 million for endowed chairs. And the Cincinnati Orchestra raised $1.75 million of its total $8 million endowment goal to endow six orchestral chairs.

Many sources make it a policy *not* to give for endowment—some foundations, for example—but corporations and individuals have supported endowment drives.

Advocacy groups can help in fund raising even though they do not raise money themselves. The Business Committee on the Arts is one such organization, and other ad hoc groups have made sizable contributions in the past. One of these was the Concerned Citizens for the Arts, founded by Amyas Ames in 1970, which assisted in gathering support for Governor Rockefeller's recommended budget for the New York State Arts Council for which the largest single sum to a state arts council—$18 million— was allocated.

Studies have shown that the American people are more concerned with the arts and humanities in the 1970s than ever before. In an editorial in *Saturday Review* John J. Veronis discussed the need for increasing federal subsidy to the arts: "More than 600 million visits are paid to American museums each year, twelve million to symphony concerts, and more than $2 billion is spent annually on cultural activities. Our painters are still the pacesetters for artists in Europe, Latin America, Australia, and Japan. Our pianists are generally considered the most technically accomplished performers in history. Our historians and literary critics are internationally renowned. Our poets dominate the entire English-speaking world. Our choreographers stage their works in London, our singers grace the stage at La Scala, our novelists are translated into Finnish and Urdu. We are a major—perhaps *the* major—cultural force today, and people everywhere should know the good news. Washington must support American artists."[6]

The cry for increased subsidies to the arts will, if heard

[6] *Saturday Review*, Apr. 22, 1972, p. 18. Note the absence of laudatory comment for theater in this listing of American achievements in the arts.

and responded to, inevitably benefit theater as well as the other performance groups. But although the patterns of increase are already apparent—between 1967 and 1972 state and territorial funding of fifty-five arts councils had grown from $2.66 million to $26.67 million—it will by no means be clear sailing.

Since federal and state funding is quixotic, dependent upon the yearly whims of Congress or legislatures, which have thus far failed to provide the real continuity of funding to their various councils and the National Endowment that might enable them to undertake long-range projects, it is entirely possible that adverse circumstances or publicity could force the position of the arts back rather than advance it. With greater subsidies from tax sources available, there will be an even greater need for scrupulous handling of and accounting for these funds.

Cash Flow

One of the most severe difficulties facing management in many theaters is handling cash-flow problems. Management must know exactly how much money is needed to assure a smooth flow of cash so that income will continue to exceed expenditure by a comfortable margin. Errors in gauging cash flow are legion among nonprofit arts organizations, even when budgets are well drawn up. As pertinent as accurate budgetary predictions are regarding exact costs of expenses to the fiscal management of the theater, the accuracy of cash-flow predictions is even more so. Commercial producers often manage cash flow by overbudgeting. A show costing $200,000 will be budgeted at $250,000, the overage providing a cushion for cash-flow needs. With this overage in hand, the producer can then return some funds to his investors even if the show flops and is closed, at which time the investors may get a 20 percent rebate. This practice builds a sense of confidence in the producer, who, after all, gave some money back!

One way of easing cash flow in a subscription-based theater is to mount the annual subscription drive in early spring. This will bring in funds at a time when cash is needed to cover commitments being negotiated for the coming fall season. This method brings in both earned and unearned income since, it is to be hoped, some subscribers will be willing to give above the price of the tickets.

The chief way of handling cash-flow problems when there is no income-producing activity is through donations. A related way is through bank loans, which obliquely involve donated funds. Bank loans can be arranged on pledges of funds from individuals or businesses or on assurance that a foundation grant or payment on a grant is imminent.

For a new venture it may be necessary to establish credit with a bank (a line of credit), and one way of doing that is to get pledges of support from various sources. For example, if a hundred wealthy patrons each pledge $10,000 of underwriting, that should assure the bank that those hundred people are willing and prepared to work diligently to see that fund-raising efforts succeed. That group of one hundred patrons could be the vital nucleus of future community support. Of course, if one individual were to give $1 million, life would be much easier. If a foundation grants that much, the amount needed from the bank could be reduced.

Pledges do not necessarily have to be fulfilled; if fund raising produces enough money from other sources on the basis of the pledges, there is no need to call them in. But since an advance commitment of donated funds is even more advantageous when a new management goes to raise funds from other sources, it might be better to ask those hundred donors for outright donations of

$1,000 each and pledged amounts of $5,000. This is to state, in effect, "We want to operate like any other businessmen: use bank loans, borrow from other sources, raise funds to cover anticipated deficits with your donations, sell tickets, undertake proper exploitation to raise money—and produce exciting theater!" If management can do what it says, there will be no need to call in the pledged money. If, however, the theater and its supporters fail to impress the public enough so that it will support the theater, then the pledgers will be liable for losses.

The chances are the pledge-makers will never be called upon for a cent. Management should emphasize a positive and appealing approach in asking help for the theater. Using the correct techniques, management should find it easier to get a hundred large pledges than a hundred large contributions. If, however, some individuals *want* to contribute rather than pledge, there is no reason to prevent them.

The ability to borrow money at the bank enables management to use other money, such as advance ticket sales, which is in trust, with impunity. It is not essential for the theater to borrow from the bank, but this may appeal to local businessmen, especially if they are given budgetary and other financial controls, which they would expect. This would be done by naming leading businessmen to the board of trustees. All pledge-makers would be offered the chance to subject the entire operation to the most searching fiscal scrutiny.

Of course, the venture can fail, usually for one of two reasons: business may not equal expectations or expenses may be higher than anticipated. If management has been successful in fund raising to that point, it will have been because the cadre of the theater has so impressed the donors, that confidence stimulated giving. A director with a reputation for accurate predictions should be able to persuade the community that he can still make accurate predictions.

In recent years several nonprofit organizations have used their tax exemption status, and even tax funds from governmental agencies, to compete commercially with Broadway theaters. Purists feel strongly that while a nonprofit theater should properly develop a potential money-making play, and it should be able to reap some reward for its labors by being paid a percentage of the earnings of any play it develops that subsequently has a successful Broadway run or is produced for film or television, that theater must not itself enter into competition with commercial producers. This is an issue that has not been fully aired in public. Such enterprising theaters as the New York Shakespeare Festival and the Long Wharf Theater have developed new plays and productions that have been transferred to commercial Broadway houses— at Broadway prices and in competition with other Broadway shows. This may be very healthy for Broadway in terms of the art of its theater, but is it a proper usage of nonprofit funds and status? Should not such funds be limited to maintaining low ticket prices to guarantee more public access? Whatever the eventual ruling or accepted practice regarding using tax-free money for what in effect is speculation, it is certain that with more governmental involvement in the arts there will be closer scrutiny.

One example of this was when the Government Accounting Office audited the books of the theater operation at the John F. Kennedy Performing Arts Center in Washington, D.C. Since the center is government-supported, the government's accountants wanted to know what was happening. They did not like what they found, and although the matter was not of major importance, it was of sufficient notoriety to produce this damaging headline in *Variety*: "See Mismanagement and Bungling First Year at Kennedy Center, D.C.; Roger Stevens Rebuts Gov't Report." The audit showed that the center had made money by covering its deficits for productions, but had actually lost money across the board on eleven productions with "an excess of revenues over production expenses of $337,000." The audit further stated that "Center productions were the consistent money losers, with Leonard Bernstein's 'Mass'—exclusive of subsequent earnings, of course . . . dropping $348,000." The matter seemed one largely of misinterpretation and Mr. Stevens replied that "the Center's budgeting and accounting system, fiercely criticized by the GAO, has been revised."[7]

Should subsidy (tax monies) be placed only in non-speculative areas of the performing arts? And what in the performing arts can really be called nonspeculative, since each production runs a risk of failure on some level? Should tax funds be spent for facilities (bricks and mortar)—nonrisk costs? However the question is decided, there will be a closer watch on the use of such funds in the future, and there is no reason why the people's money should not be spent at least as wisely in the arts as in industry, transportation, agriculture, communication, defense and other aspects of the national economy supported all or in part by tax monies.

To sum up, an RAS Theater, like any other business venture, must have substantial capital to permit long-range planning and making of commitments. Planning season-by-season is ad hoc planning and lacks efficiency, although most of our theaters have been forced to operate in this artistically limiting fashion. The ideal situation is when a single source or several—foundations, individuals, corporations—commit sufficient funds to guarantee a developmental period of several years. This

---

[7] *Variety*, Aug. 23, 1971.

has happened on occasion,[8] and the result is that managers of a project can attract a professional staff of high quality with assurance of project continuity, which in turn enables the planners to set high goals of achievement with the probability of reaching them.

[8] In 1974 the Rockefeller Foundation, having developed a concept for a Bicentennial project, acted to set up a nonprofit corporation to carry out the project. The goal was to put together and distribute free, to a large number of cultural organizations around the world, a set of 100 recordings of American music spanning the country's history, the set to be accompanied by suitable textual and visual materials. In order to guarantee the project, the Foundation's Board of Trustees indicated a willingness to commit the Foundation to the project for about four years and to put up as much as $4 million. Under these circumstances, planning was orderly, and excellent professionals were engaged.

12

The Unions:
Toward a New Understanding

NEITHER INDIVIDUALS NOR THEIR societies are naturally equitable. We must strive toward tempering injustices that are imposed on this or that segment of society by social, economic or governmental practices. Unionism in America has written some glorious chapters in human relations—and some ugly ones as well. On balance, we are a healthier nation for our vigorous labor union movement.

Originally designed to obtain improved working conditions for labor, the unions have now grown to include professional groups. In *A Theory of Justice*, John Rawls proposes that social and economic inequalities are tolerable only when they are to everyone's advantage and that each person has the right to the most extensive liberty compatible with a like liberty for others.

In a discussion of unions in relation to professional theater in the RAS concept, little can be said that will not seem vague. Reaching agreements with unions is essential for all business managements, and those agreements reflect taking into consideration current realities of the day. Therefore, it is almost impossible in a book such as this to present a clear guide to labor-management relations.

Admitting, however, that this area must be explored in real time with representatives of the various views in meetings, it can be suggested here that the RAS Theater applies its labor concepts to principles such as those enunciated by Rawls. It should be evident to the reader by this time that the RAS Theater already embodies these concepts. Let us look at an example of how the principle might work in practice. Suppose a star performer, whose undeniable magnetism grants a status which should be reflected in salary, is paid at such a high rate that wages for lesser performers are disproportionately low; the value of the star to the company becomes eroded.

Since all personnel in professional theater are represented by unions, the principle applies to all the theater's employees, the actors, directors, designers, stagehands, ticket takers, ushers, business managers.[1] In some cases, specialization within one union is so extensive that rules and regulations differ for subgroups. Resulting overspecializations and over-restrictions can become frustrating tangles for employer and employee. Many union rules cover conditions which no longer exist. Seemingly unfair union practices could be alleviated if the anachronisms were replaced by realistic agreements. This would, of course, require candor, imagination and concern for the real problems of skilled and unskilled laborers in theater. In the Rawlsian concept, advantaged or favored employees should gain from their fortunate status solely on terms that improve the situation of those who do not gain, or who lose.

With unemployment a chronic concern, what union leader would thwart the opening or operating of a theater that aimed at the employment of some 200 professionals? Indeed, the proposed conditions of RAS Theater employment should engender the active support of union leaders in the formation of the company.

[1] For a comprehensive discussion of this subject, the reader is urged to see *Labor Relations in the Performing Arts*, by Michael H. Moskow, Associated Councils on the Arts, New York, 1969.

Improving working conditions in ad hoc situations has been difficult for some unions. For example, Actors Equity, the performer's union for legitimate theater actors, has long sought to improve working conditions and wages. But it nevertheless permits actors to work for less than living wages and offers the weakest pension plan of any union in the profession. Some practices have clearly not benefited American theater; the rulings limiting the use of foreign professionals, for instance, has had the effect of preventing these skilled performers from working in American productions. The unreasonableness of this posture is underlined by the fact that in film, opera, ballet and music, American professionals have not been forced out of work by foreign talent that has been invited to participate. And the contribution of the non-Americans has enhanced those arts.

The high unemployment rate among actors is the cause for such ostracizing rulings and is also reflected in Equity's disproportionate concern with Unemployment Insurance, which is the lifeline of many American actors. In order to keep its peripatetic membership fully acquainted with the unemployment compensation laws in the various states, Equity maintains a full-time person on its staff.

Were a theater to offer a professional pay scale on an annual basis, a substantial and new tone of security would be introduced to the historically threatened professional actor and his union. It is likely, in the event such practices become standard, that actors would begin to press for the tenured situations their European counterparts enjoy and which musicians' unions here have approached in their symphonic agreements. That is an issue to be anticipated and resolved at an appropriate time.

Not unrelated to the concept of tenure is that of feather-bedding. As fervent as my wish is that none should work in theater without adequate compensation, I am equally opposed to payment for workers whose services are not required. No rationale exists today for featherbedding. Neither sub-subsistence nor unearned wages can nourish the cooperative spirit and sense of true equity to which the RAS Theaters must be dedicated.

Theory on this point has been developed and I subscribe to economist Edward E. Lawler III's position that, "pay in fact can motivate people, but only within the context of an open and democratically run corporation. Research indicates that salaries will affect the productivity of employees if certain conditions hold: If pay rates respond to current individual performances; if salary information is public; if employees participate with managers in evaluating their own performances; if managers are willing to explain and justify salary policy to employees."[2] The problem in any merit pay system is how to measure performance. Criteria for judgment must be valid for management and workers, and should lead to promotion and pay decisions acceptable to all. "Mutual trust can be established only with mutual influence; that is, an employee should feel that he has a real opportunity to influence his boss, as well as the other way around."[3]

The cooperative spirit pervading basic agreements should inform special projects as well. Since theater professionals are increasingly aware of the potentials of television, the RAS Theater management must plan on being involved in television and film projects as a matter of course. These projects will be foci of union negotiations. An example of a form of approach is illustrated in the following excerpt from a proposal worked out and presented to the labor unions of the Metropolitan Opera in 1970 and in which I attempted to deal with *anticipated issues*:

"This [Electronic Project] memorandum is to sum-

[2] Edward E. Lawler III, "Does Money Make People Work Harder?", *Yale Alumni Magazine*, April 1968.
[3] Lawler, ibid.

marize areas to be considered *before* preparing an agenda of items to be discussed with the unions in connection with a proposed joint venture in the field of electronics (i.e., records, cassettes, video tapes, etc.).

Purpose of Joint Venture. It is our understanding that the major objectives of this project are threefold:

(a) to obtain additional sources of revenue;

(b) to provide an additional source of income for Metropolitan employees and thereby lessen their dependence upon it as a primary source of earnings;

(c) to find a common ground for discussion and work with the union employees and thereby improve labor relations."

The memorandum proposed that the project be "a joint venture between the Metropolitan and the unions." The Met would supply venture capital and the unions, insofar as possible, would supply the services of their employees *free of charge.* "The products will be marketed," the memo went on, "and after the Metropolitan has recouped its initial risk capital, revenue derived from the sale of recordings, etc., will be divided in an agreed-upon proportion between the Metropolitan and the unions."

The proposal succeeded in setting a tone and pattern for future cooperation, replacing management-employee divisiveness with partnership goals for extra-income activity. The principles, accepted by the key unions at the Met, have not been implemented.

The theater that intends to serve a large community must be sensitive to all aspects of labor-management problems. To ignore or deal unimaginatively with these issues is to court disaster before a first curtain has risen. Unions, as protective representatives of their memberships, understandably seek the most advantageous terms. It has been my experience that unions will modify or change rules, pay scales and conditions when convinced there is cause. Amicable solutions to labor-management relationships can be fostered if an atmosphere of caring and mutual respect exists for the problems and positions inherent in the stratified worlds of each.

With the creation of RAS Theaters, difficulty should be obviated as management is able to say to and with the unions, let us leave behind the rules of an itinerant theater; a new concept needs new rules based only on living wages, fair working conditions and stimulating artistic rewards benefiting all. In setting working conditions for the first years of operation, it must further be realized that they may not be applicable ten years hence. Therefore, no condition, on either side, must be regarded as a sacred precedent that precludes subsequent reevaluation.

13

The Board:
The Power's the Thing

THE SEAT OF ULTIMATE power in any organization is in its board of directors. The board is the financial dynamo which switches on the lights of the RAS Theater through its decisions, fund raising, selection of administrator or artistic director, approval of policy and budget. Managers, directors and actors come and go, but boards have a way of staying on.

The formation of the board is perhaps a more important organizational step than any other save the naming of the artistic head. The organizers of the theater must carefully consider potential members not only as individuals, but also as representatives of various fields and social strata. There must be a healthy balance of opinion and expertise on the board initially, because what is created initially may persist. Boards tend to perpetuate themselves: a banker is succeeded by another banker, a lawyer by a lawyer, the rich by the rich.

The record of board achievements in a number of non-profit organizations is dismal, in some cases disastrous. A few case histories will demonstrate perhaps the worst side of nonprofit board actions and promote the case for organizing boards on more democratic lines.

André Gregory, a brilliant young director, was told by veteran director Alan Schneider to "go to the regionals" for experience, rather than hang around Broadway. This was in the 1960s when regional theater was getting some patronage and an excited press. Gregory went to Philadelphia and became managing director of the Theater of the Living Arts. His reign was dazzling but brief. In 1967 he was dismissed by his board. Earlier that same year another bright director, John Hancock (who later directed the successful film *Bang the Drum Slowly*), had been dismissed from the Pittsburgh Playhouse directorship by his board and Herbert Blau had left the Lincoln Center Repertory Theater.

Theater critics were livid. What were these know-nothing boards doing to good artists? Martin Gottfried of *Women's Wear Daily* called Gregory's dismissal "the final straw in an all too predictable pattern of stupid behavior by resident theater boards of trustees. The expelling of Mr. Gregory was the third such resident theater act of violence in the past month."

Gregory was appreciated by his board and that made the firing the more absurd. "Gregory was fired," Gottfried said, "in an emotionally heated situation that really had nothing to do with his theater policies. What happened was that David Lunney, the company's executive director, was refused a contract, took this as a vote of no-confidence and resigned. Gregory liked Lunney and had worked with him. Hoping to get Lunney back, he suspended activities as artistic director. The board then fired him. . . ."

John Hancock, according to Gottfried, had been forced to alter the planned season of serious plays to include commercial and "cheap" plays. He had to announce publicly that he would try to program plays "that would appeal to everybody." Gottfried mistakenly thought the board should have taken over the subscription department and audience-developing programs, a clear function of management.

Herbert Blau, then jointly directing the Lincoln Center Repertory Theater with Jules Irving, had directed a season of plays and written some articles of a political nature that caused the board to lose confidence in him. He resigned and several commercial productions were booked into the Vivian Beaumont Theater until the Repertory Theater was re-formed under Irving.

Henry Hewes, the theater critic for *Saturday Review*, said of the triple firing in 1967 that there was a danger of resident companies becoming too tame because of the pressure on them to please their boards of directors, their sources of financial support.

The single worst danger in board-management conflicts is not dismissals but the inhibition of artistic management. As a theater's leadership becomes cowed, the theater becomes duller. A prime example of theater board-management controversy was New York's Lincoln Center Repertory Theater. This board, formed before the company was created, had in 1962 hired Elia Kazan and Robert Whitehead, who were undermined by the board after three years and replaced by Jules Irving and Herbert Blau. The latter left in 1967 after two years. Irving announced his resignation midway in the 1972–1973 season, charging that his board had failed to raise funds to ensure the experimental season at the Forum Theater downstairs, and that there were points beyond which he would not compromise. The board at one point considered announcing bankruptcy and giving back a portion of subscription funds. But the negative impact of such reneging on the subscribers of other Lincoln Center houses—the New York Philharmonic, the Metropolitan Opera, the New York City Ballet and Opera—sobered the board into muddling through the season, although the splendid Forum season was cut off after the highly acclaimed Beckett Festival.

The board's first plan was to reorganize the whole theater, beginning with the board itself, and a special Lincoln Center committee was established to do the study on reorganization. The fear among many knowledgeable theater professionals was that the theater would again become a booking house for commercial attractions while the reorganization took place, and that the Repertory Theater might simply fade away.

Blame for all the Lincoln Center Repertory Theater's shortcomings has been mistakenly placed on the head of Jules Irving, a manager with the blind perseverance to work within the hopeless strictures placed on him by high labor costs, small staff and company budgets.

A source of the long, frustrating problems at the Beaumont, according to playwright Arthur Miller, was that "the Lincoln Center board *never* intended to have a repertory theater—a theater doing several productions at the same time—and they don't intend to now because they cannot and will not supply the money for repertory." The board had given Whitehead an okay on a building without establishing a budget on how much money would be allotted for the building, how much for salaries. The board's "great giants of industry, banking and commerce," said Miller, "can't get it through their heads that the more successful a repertory theater is, the more it must cost." Why did the board choose Blau and Irving? "I figured," said Miller, "the board looked around and said, 'Who is loved?' and found Irving and Blau, poor fellows." This, because the New York critics had been hard on Kazan and Whitehead. "But the answer," Miller continued, "is simpler, I think. They'd be cheaper than Whitehead, who was not trying to build a San Francisco repertory company but something in America that would vie with the great companies of the world." Miller recommended that the critics realize the board's culpability, because "this is a public business. It's not entirely the board's business how Lincoln Center is run, because public money is involved and it's New York's land, our property they're sitting on. . . . You will never have a repertory company so long as that board is in control and that is where the critics should make their attack, carefully and coolly."[1]

These were prophetic words. Miller sounds a theme here which could bear amplification. The nonprofit board serves as a public trust. Since this is so, there is every reason to avoid past patterns of board organizations and form the RAS Theater board along new patterns.

For the RAS Theater to relate to the community fully, the board must have true community representation, not just the leading business and civic leaders. For the theater to relate to itself, the board must have staff representation, not just the manager and his business staff. The employees—artists and craftsmen—should be represented on the board. Before approving any specific nominee for the board, the first consideration should be what group or interest the person represents that can broaden the scope of the theater's administrative arm, and what that person can bring to the board through his outside affiliations.

Boards of directors can be angels or albatrosses. Unfortunately too many are weak, ineffectual or counterproductive.

Nonprofit organizations (NPOs) must, by law, have boards of directors, and these can have as few as three members or as many as the organization feels are needed. Somewhere between fifteen and fifty is the average for large organizations. NPOs came into existence some time ago, but in the theater they are of fairly recent birth. NPO board structure tends to follow corporate patterns of makeup and exercise of power. The profit board is influenced by the leading stockholders, who frequently dictate who will sit. Dissenters are usually forced

[1] Symposium in *Dramatist Guild Quarterly*, reprinted in *The New York Times*, Apr. 12, 1972.

to leave (if they are unable to gain power) to make room for others who are sympathetic to the majority which appoints them.

NPO boards own no shares and are not paid for sitting. Each has an equal vote and minority opinions can be registered with impunity, although they rarely are. When members leave the board, they are replaced, usually through a nominating procedure under a nominating committee of the board. Board leaderships are interested in maintaining control and therefore seek replacements that perpetuate the board's original makeup. NPO boards have followed this policy and since most are composed of nonartists or now specialists in the field of the organization (in this case, theater), self-perpetuation generally fails to give the organization an informed board. It is helpful in funding an NPO to have social and business leaders on the board, but there is no reason why boards must be unbalanced. It is true that the civic leaders lend an air of solidity and respectability to the board and the organization, which artists or professionals may lack in the eyes of the community. But why not have both?

Boards are supposed to do at least five things: (1) hire or appoint a head of the organization, (2) approve the program of operation, (3) approve the budget for operation, (4) raise money and (5) judge the end result. In actual practice the most important work a board can do is number (4)—*raise money!* Finding the administrator is important too, and if he is worthy and if sufficient funds have been brought in to balance his deficit-projected budget, the other three functions of the board will be simply routine. Most boards, when they fail, fail because they have not found artistic leadership and/or raised enough money. When such failure occurs, boards find themselves tangled in the internal affairs of the theater, namely making the budget or establishing artistic policy and overseeing the production of the plays themselves. When this kind of involvement happens, the organization is in deep trouble. But it happens, and usually because incompetence produced an unplanned deficit —not the budgeted deficit—which exceeded a reasonable limit; because of lack of confidence in management due to other reasons; because of lack of sympathy with management's goals; because some board members have a keener sense of self-aggrandizement than service.

A delicate relationship exists between the board and the theater, one that is constantly in flux. There are some passionate, public-spirited persons who can alleviate problems in an organization by their bright leadership, personal contributions or their ability to persuade others to give. But because a negative board leadership can cause real problems, attention should be focused there. The inferior board chairman might dominate the artistic director and thus inhibit the organization's artistic growth by limiting funds or appeasing nonprofessional whims; on the other hand, a charismatic director may steamroll the board into decisions or policies beyond the community's ability to absorb them. The strength of each division—the board and management—must be constantly tested. In battles for power it is usually the chairman of the board who wins, since the board has hiring and firing power over management. The value of an individual such as Mrs. August Belmont, whose leadership and passionate devotion blessed the cause of opera before and during my tenure at the Metropolitan, cannot be overestimated. Never content with the status quo, she endlessly searched for new answers and new directions to old problems and to challenges of the future. Although her unique gifts cannot be duplicated, an active search must be instigated for the cultivated and artistically alert of each community, whose ability to translate interest into action can readily be mobilized.

Boards are exclusive clubs and there are dues to be

paid. In prestigious organizations board membership is a prized social or business plum and positions can be earned, bought or inherited. The mystique of honor and status conferred by board membership dictates that no one rock the boat. Such blueblood boards are found in major museums, symphony orchestras, opera and ballet companies, and they like to surround themselves with their own kind. Blueblood boards often look for managers or artistic directors who are members of their group, or at the very least are nonembarrassing to them.

Since the social upheaval of the 1960s, however, a quiet revolution has been taking place in the NPO boardrooms where one will now find women, Jews, Latins, Italians, blacks and Irish Catholics on what were predominantly WASP organizations (though some still persist in their old ways). This is to the good, for the dominant arts organizations have not in the past reflected the multiethnic hue of America.

Forming the board can be done prior to or after legal incorporation. In some instances organizers of a project get their seed money first, then try to put together a board; in others they do both at once. Or, a board of civic leaders can form itself and, in order to accomplish some desirable task, incorporate and look for a management.

The ideal situation is where the artistic director forms the company and chooses the board. How should he choose? Since many problems of arts organizations stem from poorly formed or functioning boards, it would be wise to think anew.

Although the recently admitted ethnic voices to NPO boards are at last giving representation to long-silent segments of the population, they do not represent the most important and significant elements of the corporate structure—the employees themselves. But who has a more direct concern with the continued functioning of the organization? They utilize about 75 percent of the organization's revenues in compensation and rightfully deserve a role in board policy-making (which controls their livelihoods) as well as a voice in the artistic decisions.

Most existing boards, however, still view employees as a threat to their continued existence, their control over the power of decision. One president of a major NPO got very upset when I mildly suggested that an employee be seated on the board. That board numbered more than forty and the idea was put forth to promote labor peace, on the theory that if the employees had one of their own on the board, he could act as a trustworthy reporter and representative, thereby narrowing the gulf separating labor and management. The idea generated hostility all around the board, whose members feared the employee would learn the board's "secrets." Had the "snooping" employee been seated, of course, his voice could have been drowned by the tidal wave of a huge majority.

Although some board members may have little background in the arts, they seldom allow modesty to inhibit their exercise of artistic judgment. Such members will, without due provocation from management, arrogate to themselves artistic control. Such takeovers spell disaster.

Rather than follow the old patterns, the RAS Theater should set a new course by setting up a board in which power is shared among civic nonprofessionals and company members. A template for such a board could be the following:

A board of twenty-five would be initially assembled, eleven coming from employee ranks, those members to include the manager, stage director and another member of the administrative staff; three directors elected by the performers; a playwright; a member elected by nonperforming personnel; and three members elected from and by the craft and service personnel. The fourteen nontheater members would come from civic, economic, cultural and public-interest organizations. The local city council could elect a few board members, or the mayor could appoint one; the local trades council and/or labor unions and university or college presidents could each elect one; several other arts groups in the city could elect one to represent their organizations; subscribers could place a member on the board to represent the interests of the audience; and the news media could elect one member.

This scheme would not rule out the two or three important fund-raising board members. And should such a board even attempt to follow the old pattern of self-perpetuation, it would have started life as broadly based as possible.

Labor leaders have occasionally sat on NPO boards, the best example probably being when Harry Van Arsdale, then head of the Central Labor Council of New York, sat on the board of Lincoln Center for the Performing Arts. This respected leader, however, had no direct contact with the various employees working for the Lincoln Center constituents. Although he was a labor leader, his work was so distant from direct operations at Lincoln Center that he was almost nonrepresentative!

Forming a board democratically is a practical matter that could be acted upon by existing arts organizations. This plan takes into account the need for artistic independence of management, the need for employee representation on the board and the responsibility to the public for fund raising and the handling of tax-exempt funds that should guarantee the corporation's financial integrity.

I further suggest that the RAS Theater set another new course for theater by vesting the technical *ownership* of the company primarily in the employees themselves. The rationale is this: Where performers collaborate to create an art and are, furthermore, the very essence of that art, which is created anew at each performance, why should the organization—which exists because of performers and which benefits sometimes quite substantially from the economic exploitation of theatrical properties generated by performance activity—not be owned by the artists who in fact create the art? The cooperative venture is a fact of American society from apartment houses to orchestras. Communal theaters of small proportions and scope have tried this. What is being called for is a more massive demonstration of the principle of employee ownership.

Orchestral musicians here and abroad have experimented with the plan with some success. London's New Philharmonia is a cooperative; the chairman of the board was at one time the principal trumpet player. The players elected eight members to serve on the board and the board chose its chairman. The orchestra, through the board, hires a business manager and decides on the artistic (musical) director. All the players hold shares, which they obtain when they join. The Vienna Philharmonic operates in a similar fashion, and these two great symphonic ensembles have functioned with great distinction. The cooperative nature of the venture has not been reflected in poor choices of musical directors. Indeed, musicians themselves are less likely to base these choices on superficial qualities.

The Boston Philharmonic, a large American chamber orchestra, imitated the foreign model. Thomas F. Ellerbe, Jr., president of the Cooperative Foundation, said in 1972 that this was one of the few such organizations in America. Most organizations in the arts are incorporated under the Nonprofit Corporation Act or are owned and operated by foundations. Such NPOs gain tax benefits as well as tax deductibility of gifts and grants from donors.

Cooperatives, however, have none of these privileges. They are private, not public, corporations and have no special gift-tax status. A cooperative is set apart from other profit-making organizations, however, in that it agrees to return any net margins above cost of operation —so-called profits—to the users or customers in proportion to each one's contribution to the business volume. This return is called a "patronage refund."

Forming the RAS Theater as a cooperative, therefore, would deny some forms of unearned income, or at least reduce the possibility of receiving funds from agencies which must grant only to tax-exempt organizations. The typical nonprofit board becomes involved in fund-raising. Therefore, a suggested solution would be for the RAS corporation to be organized along the nonprofit lines indicated, and then to make a contract with the employees, who could be exclusively organized into a cooperative. This would mean two organizations: one nonprofit, which would own the real estate and handle the general public service aspects; and a second, which would be the performing group and share in the by-products or monies gained from the useful exploitation of the art, such as from television, film and the like.

Because distinguished board members are hard to find, cynicism marks nonprofit parlance. For example, there is the comment attributed to a curator of the Metropolitan Museum of Art in New York: "I've never seen a good trustee." Architect Philip Johnson once said, "When a museum is functioning smoothly, there's almost nothing for a trustee to do." When asked what to look for in a trustee, Johnson said, "Money." When pressed further, the answer was, "That's three things. Money, money, money." A board president, however, voiced more common criteria: "The three W's: Wealth. Wisdom. Work."[2]

The area of board responsibility is vast. The least visible part of a major theater's operation, it can be a buoyant

[2] Quotes from Sophy Burnham, "The Manhattan Arrangement of Art and Money," *New York*, Dec. 1969.

lifesaver or that portion of the iceberg which dooms a *Titanic*. It cannot be overemphasized that boards must be carefully formed. Rules of operation should be clear. Causes for firing board members should be stated. Board membership should be limited to a period of years with an obligatory off-period before being seated again (the period on could be five or ten years, the off-time two or four years). Three-year cycles would permit sitting for two cycles, and leaving for one cycle. Regressive self-perpetuation must be ended on nonprofit boards. Among the wealthy in any metropolitan area there is usually a key entity, a person, a family or association, which would be helpful in attracting others to the theater. There would be no need for an equal-status board—in fact, including employee representatives makes that impossible—but there is no reason to ostracize the wealthy. Quite the contrary! Some board members would join because of community spirit, and they might be representatives of various specialties— a librarian, a writer, retired performers. One could reasonably expect about three sparkplugs on the board, members who work enthusiastically and with good wishes for the theater. Often a retired businessman with an interest in theater will invest the same energies and concentration that brought him to the top of his field in the service of the theater. He would be, then, a most valuable trustee.

There are no absolute rules about board members and their ability to function well. Wealth and education do not guarantee taste and learning, nor do they ensure a lack of it. Personality determines a given board member's value to the theater. Possession of the three W's should be the keys to board membership and involvement. A manager of a small theater company might feel secure working with a small board. The smaller the board, the easier it might be for its members to agree, but this may not be desirable from a professional point of view. A large board would have more differences of opinion and management might be able to effect beneficial ties with key members without incurring the wrath of others. Few managements seek the active participation of the board in running the organization, however. A large board with one yearly meeting fairly well guarantees a minimum of interference. In such cases the manager would probably work closely with the executive committee and the board officers, advising them of all impending crises and problems. It is essential that the manager have good relations with this, the working portion of the board.

The artistic director must be given his head and the board should not act as a drag on him. The independent Broadway producer has more freedom in this respect, for he is responsible only to his investors, to whom he owes merely an accounting for funds received. The nonprofit manager, however, is free to persuade his board that he knows best. Indeed, this is part of his job and an important management technique.

The artistic director must avoid disappointing the expectations of the board. When troubles arise—slipping income, poor subscription, loss of quality technical or artistic staff—the board must be informed quickly. Boards do not like confrontations or surprises. They do not like reading unexpected bad news in the papers. Management's key rule should be: "Let the board know about potential trouble as long in advance as possible." The board's credo should be: "Back the director you have chosen." And the director must realize that the board rarely loses an argument; he might be right, but if a majority of the board votes him wrong, he's wrong.

Approving a budget—a board function—involves fund raising, since a predicted deficit will be part of the budget. A central question in approving each deficit budget will be: Do we raise the prices, or get more money from outside? If management has as a prime goal a low-ticket-price policy, the question should be resolved in favor of that policy. Approving the budget entails problem solving, and board members should be chosen with that in mind. With professional representation from the company on the board, the noncompany members can be people who have shown they can solve problems of all sorts. A Nobel Prize–winning geneticist can become a distinguished president of a university. Teachers can become good executives. Individuals can change careers and achieve greater success. Many people have perception and wisdom in matters outside their specialties. Problem solvers possess transferable skills to a high degree.

Conflict must inevitably arise in any human society, regardless of how great the mutual understanding of technical, emotional, intellectual and financial matters. Although the techniques for handling management-labor disagreements are well known, those for coping with board-management problems scarcely exist. Mediation (an attempt to reconcile both sides, in which no decisions are binding) and arbitration (in which conflicts are resolved expeditiously by a third party) might be imported from labor-management relations. Bringing in an outside negotiator would enable warring factions to simmer down and temper their passionate discussions with reason.

The board should be able to set its own goals, and be conscious of its own need for intellectual rejuvenation, the better to serve its organization. An example of good leadership in this area is shown by a memo circulated to the Lincoln Center constituents in April 1971 by Lincoln Center President Amyas Ames. In it he brought up important questions about the role of Lincoln Center and its future directions. He functioned then in the best tradition of a board chairman. The questions were practical, to the point: (1) What should be the role of Lincoln Center in this new world of the 1970s? (2) Looking back over the first ten years, when has the separate entity which we call Lincoln Center, Inc., failed? (3) What are the successes of Lincoln Center? (4) How can we best use the income from our endowment? (5) Which of these activities should be given the highest priority: Communications (television, film, etc., use of the proposed "culture channels"), Community Relations, International University Program, Networks of Arts Centers, Lincoln Center Press (a central publishing project for all the constituents) and Programming (interconstituential programming involving retrospectives of composers, artists, celebrations, anniversaries, etc.)?

These were broad questions intended to prod long-range thinking from organizations busy with daily problems. This kind of reflective nudging is appropriate from a board.

In drawing up its contract with management, the board should delegate authority to the administrators for periods of perhaps three to five years. The contract should contain an artistic control clause which clearly says, "The administration has sole artistic control." In dealing with the management it would be wise for the board to press for the following rules: (1) All major problems should be communicated to the board. (2) The board must be warned before an important position is filled or vacated through resignation or firing. (3) The board must be consulted on all decisions concerning quality control. (4) Management must not exceed the budgets for the season, although the budgets for individual productions may well change after being set. (5) Management should include some plays in the season that are contrary to its own point of view.

Rules should be set and adhered to, but the wise person knows when to set the rule book aside, for a greater value. The phrase "distinguished disobedience" was given recognition by the Empress Maria Theresa of Austria by a special award. The great admiral, Lord Nelson, practiced distinguished disobedience and became a legendary hero when he put the telescope to his blind eye. And there will come a time when a manager will have to practice distinguished disobedience and thwart his board's rules. Let us hope, for the future of the RAS Theaters in America, that when that time comes, the board will have on hand one of Maria Theresa's awards.

14

Morality and Taste

MORALITY IS COMPOSED OF actions, taste of choices. The RAS Theater so far described is one of high moral tone, conceived as a nonprofit cooperative theater dedicated to the community that brings it into being. The theater brings employment opportunities and artistic pleasure to the community. The functioning of the management, the board, the dealings with labor, the handling of staff problems, have been described as necessitating a spirit of cooperation and understanding among individuals of strong minds and wills. The selection of the repertory and the use of the theaters should emphasize social realities and issues. Providing room for dissent within the theater's repertory is important. The theater's leaders should also take the position that this theater is not theirs, but that they hold a public trust. It may be a theater of high artistic caliber, but in the best sense it should be a people's theater. The recommended structure of the board militates toward an enlightened populism. The theater is needed not only to serve a community but also to help save a valuable profession from continuing in a degraded state. When the decision is taken to pay actors living wages under long-term arrangements and to offer them artistically stimulating and personally rewarding work, the action resulting from such a decision is a moral one and should be beneficial to many, not just a few.

Although the RAS Theater is about art, it is also about being humane. One profession—theater—has been isolated for treatment. The art form involved in theater is important to man, although this importance has been neglected in American society. Nevertheless, the ubiquity of theater may be its best rationale for existing. No art can lay claim to biological necessity. But so basic is theater, the dramatic, make-believe impulse, to every age and time that one must grant it a prominent place in the hierarchy of human consciousness. The experience of theater is so well known it needs little explanation or excuse for being. Because of theater's power to grip the imagination and work upon the reflective mind, to expunge hidden fears, to externalize a complex of feelings and in so doing to relieve their pressure (the well-known cathartic effect), theater has been embraced and supported by all the peoples of the world. American theater as currently practiced on Broadway and in nonprofit theaters around the country is a welfare profession. Unemployment is the constant. There is no inherent reason why the art of theater should not enjoy the economic protection in America that the art of music has received. A decision to try to stimulate that protection is a moral one. Valuing the performer over the play is a moral choice.

There can be no attempt to set artistic standards in a book. In theater or any art, that can only be done *in situ* by artists. But broad questions of what kind of emphasis the RAS Theater should place on its organization, its repertory and the treatment of plays and performers can be discussed.

A major theater should provide good theater. But what is good theater? Ten artists may give ten answers, all different. Perhaps the question should be: What effect will this theater have on the people who work in it and

attend its performances? Will it have a beneficial effect
on their lives? How will it affect their ideas, attitudes,
psychology? Will it raise their level of social, intellectual
and esthetic awareness? Will the theater experience be
entertaining merely, will it assault the audience's minds
and senses and provide no nourishment? Will it be a
balm for weary souls, a source of encouragement for
the dispirited? Should the theater only mirror the society,
or should it try to point a way to a better one? Is it pre-
tentious to even pose such a question, or is this not what
Lorca was talking about when he said, "A theater which
in every branch, from tragedy to vaudeville, is sensitive
and well-oriented, can in a few years change the sensi-
bility of a people"?

The RAS Theater, while aimed at the egregious problems of the profession, must likewise be aimed at its
audience, and not merely to sell tickets. Can a theater be
artistically elitist and at the same time populist? Why
not? Through stimulating performance of great plays a
theater should be able to stimulate a community. This is
not meant to confuse art with sociology, but to realize that,
just as every economic decision in the theater involves an
artistic decision, so all artistic and economic decisions are
moral.

What of taste in presenting plays? What are the limits
of what an open-minded director or playwright can ask of
an open-minded audience? The unprecedented period of
theatrical freedom that marked the 1960s and was a part
of the sexual revolution seems to have reached a peak.
In the early 1970s, however, one could still put anything
on the stage so long as it did not provoke panic in the
theater.

Robert Brustein has commented that "the public is willing to sit still for representations that a few years ago
might have issued in complaints, warrants, or riots. Permissiveness in regard to sexual activity in the theater has

been extended to everything short of actual copulation, and for the first time in almost 2,500 years it is possible to satirize the highest leaders of government on stage without fear of physical harm or legal retribution."[1] The Living Theater did actually invite audience members to copulate with actors following one performance at the Brooklyn Academy in 1968.

If some reveled in this new libertinism, others reacted negatively. The fear was not of frankness itself, but of the Frankenstein monster that can lurk in pornography, of its dehumanizing and depersonalizing qualities. As pornography and censorship were poised against each other— with battles being fought over films such as *Deep Throat* —arguments were heated on both sides. We seem unable to agree on what pornography is. Is sexuality obscene, or is violence the true obscenity? If there are redeeming social values, is the play, film or novel not pornographic? Who can agree what constitutes a redeeming social value? The Supreme Court decision to relegate to communities the decisions over what constitutes pornography and to let them ban what they choose is one way out, but is it the most democratic?

Pornography raises not only legal and moral but psychological issues as well. The theater must take into account this delicate subject for it will be a *bête noire* until firm policy is forged. An example of the ironies of the issue is seen in one New York situation. Theaters around Times Square exerted some pressure on the city to close pornographic film and bookstores in the area. "It was not too many years ago," wrote Harvard lawyer Alan M. Dershowitz to the editor of *The New York Times*, "that some legitimate theaters themselves were being closed down because of allegedly pornographic performances. (Indeed, it was as recently as 1970 that I participated in

[1] *The New Republic*, May 6, 1972.

a legal defense of the play *Hair* when it was banned in Boston.)" The theaters in question had tolerated the porno shops until they became "too raunchy," and their clientele's depressing effect on the Times Square environs began to "affect their own profits." Dershowitz warned against closing down the porno shops for, he wrote, "while it may serve the short-term interests of the residents of Times Square, the lesson of history has been that in the long run, a regime of censorship is far more dangerous to the values we all share." I agree.

Like most moral problems, this one requires choosing between two rights rather than a right and a wrong. Little is known of the actual effects of pornography on people. One writer suggests that it is not "the existence of stage sex shows or explicit films or perverted sexual activity that matters so much" as the widespread "attitude that nothing is wrong with such displays—and what matters more is that liberal people even assume they are beneficial." He cites the report of President Nixon's Commission on Pornography in which one writer is quoted as saying that there is "no evidence that we needed protection from the exploitation of our fantasy."[2] Not to be sure of how to handle pornography is one thing, not to know whether it is good or bad for one is another.

Many claim that pornography brutalizes values and that "only by adhering to a strictly behaviourist and reductionist view of man can we maintain our bland view of the harmlessness of pornography. If we accept the realities of meaning and values . . . there must be deep human objections."[3]

My bias toward a conservatism which is free of censorship is expressed by J. B. Priestley, who wrote, "Sex needs to be described from the inside as a poet or novelist can

[2] David Holbrook, "The Dehumanising of Sex," *The Guardian*, Sept. 16, 1972.
[3] *Ibid.*

do, and when it is shown from the outside, with solid bodies on the stage, we are turned into voyeurs . . . . Moreover, I feel that by putting a premium on shock tactics, you tempt a young playwright away from the hard work of creating a true and satisfying piece of life . . . and encourage him to write something thin and half-finished but startling."[4]

As the song says, "What the world needs now is love, sweet love." An RAS Theater can have a loving effect on a community depending on whether management has what a London *Times* critic called "a taste for decadence and moral inversion," or an appetite for humanization. The plays, policies, actors, board, all will cast ballots for or against a destructive permissiveness. The decision will never be easy, but the question must be prominently asked.

Commenting on the lack of moral fiber in American theater, Tyrone Guthrie once said that merely because legitimate theater has ceased to be "the dominant means of distribution, we must not conclude that it may not still be a dominant source of ideas." The death of theater is not imminent. It has always faced changing times by evolving new forms. It is active, not static, even as film and television are. Guthrie railed against the moral laxity of our theaters and leaders by saying that "at present we are simply fooling around with this primitive and powerful means of expression. We have, largely through lack of philosophy of drama, effected its arbitrary and unnatural divorce from religion and from most of the serious ideas of both our private and public lives." To Guthrie, we rarely value theater more highly than as "a frivolous pastime, principally devoted to erotic titillation." The result of this public attitude has been the vulgarization of the art of theater. "There is no clear distinction," Sir Tyrone said, "between what is offered as a

---

[4] J. B. Priestley, "Old Stager," *The Guardian*, April 20, 1924.

serious expression of thought and feeling, and what is offered solely as a diversion, and to make money.["5]
The RAS Theater would make the distinction in its repertory approach. Values are created by the search for values. That theater serves art best which creates an original style, develops an original idea or helps shape an original mind to its best accomplishments. A theater of imitation is an affront to an infinitely varied universe, to unique fingerprints, one-of-a-kind snowflakes. The theater that sings a song none has sung contributes much, whether the contribution be received or not.

A contribution can be vastly out of proportion to the size of the theater. The National Theater of the Deaf, organized at the Eugene O'Neill Memorial Theater Center at Waterford, Connecticut, by David Hays, is an original theater for all audiences. It performs traditional plays with hearing actors narrating what the mute actors act, mime or "sign." Audiences seeing this unique theater are moved, never out of pity. They perceive a depth of communication, a clarity of emotional and psychological probity frequently absent from hearing actors. Sign language, one realizes, is not just an abstract pattern of hand movements, but a choreography of human feeling in which the word "meeting" is interpreted "my heart goes out to you," by the hand leading from the heart to the person "met."

The artistic revolution that began in the 1960s has, in its course of conflict between personal and societal values, bred small theaters of highly creative impact. Experimental theaters and those rooted in communal experimentation have included Joseph Chaikin's Open Theater, Jerzy Grotowski's Polish Laboratory Theater, the Living Theater, the Magic Theater of Omaha, Richard Schechner's Performance Group, and various La Mama

5 Tyrone Guthrie, *In Various Directions*, New York, The Macmillan Company, 1965, p. 211.

companies. These theaters often were more interested in process than product and that process involved the actor's life full-time. The credos of these groups were reminiscent of the Group Theater's manifesto in the 1930s proclaiming that the intellectual and moral life of the participants was equal to their artistic work.

Writing almost forty years later, Richard Schechner could echo the goals of the Group Theater. To him and others in the movement, the movement was all. It could be a rebellious movement, but the basis of its art was living together in harmony. In a *New York Times* piece entitled "Want to Watch or Act?" Schechner summed up the feelings of many when he wrote, "In varying degrees many of the new theaters are communities. They try to give their members more than employment or even a place where art can flourish. Grotowski speaks of his theater in religious terms, of 'novitiates' and 'disciples.' The Living Theater is an acknowledged floating community whose art comes from the community life. The Open Theater and the Performance Group believe that life style and performing style are not separable."

For these artists there was no distinction between art and life—a concept shared by primitive societies and one to which perhaps American culture may evolve. Just as the theater artists stressed *being* over *training*—"One simply cannot be a great performer and a lousy human being," a statement open to debate, unfortunately—so graphic artists, searching for values beyond the traditional gallery situation espoused *being* over *product*. Critic Harold Rosenberg echoed the anguished cries of gallery owners that the artist was no longer interested in the art object. Artists had "passed beyond art and become artists in a pure state." The artist, in this view, was greater than the work of art, and the value of the object presumably diminished in relationship to the greatness of the artist. Rosenberg wrote, "The post-art artist carries the definition of art to the point where nothing is left of art but the fiction of the artist. He disdains to deal in anything but essences. Instead of dance, poetry, film, he deals in movement; instead of music, he deals in sound. He has no need for art since by definition the artist is a man of genius and what he does 'would,' in [Andy] Warhol's phrase, naturally, 'come out as art.' "[6]

While the retreat of artists into a semimystical search for essence may frustrate the public, is it not a mirror of American society's own search for new values in a life-style made arid through dehumanization, technology and loss of the simple ability to communicate?

The artist, with antennae into the future (or is it as Edgard Varèse said: Artists are not ahead of their times, it's just that people are behind theirs?), truly holds up the mirror to society. For an index to American political upheaval and ground-level changes in collective concepts, examine the upheavals in the arts for the period just preceding the change. So much of what has become a world life-style began with a literary–life-style movement epitomized by Jack Kerouac and his *On the Road*, and the later flower children and hippies who came out of San Francisco's love-drug culture. The cutting edge of social movements are in the arts, painting, music, dress, dancing.

In order to serve its audience the RAS Theater must be a homing ground for artists of many styles. If the theater's professional standards insist on skills not attained by communal troupes or their actors, that does not mean those groups cannot be invited to perform at the theater. And just because it is unwilling to freeze art into a museum exhibition does not mean the theater must abandon the dramatic literature of the past. New styles, new plays, new playwrights, talented performers, all must be

[6] Harold Rosenberg, *On the De-Definition of Art*, Associated Councils of the Arts report, reprint, Jan. 1972.

nurtured by the theater. A new idea should be entertained so long as it has a positive human value. The theater will have made a contribution to the profession and the community when it has produced something of value to others.

An RAS Theater in Baltimore, Cleveland, Denver or Phoenix must think anew, search itself for its own community values and find ways of giving those values and aspirations expression. Imitation can be prelude to innovation, for each generation stands on the shoulders of its parents. One problem with regional theaters has been, as David Merrick, the Broadway producer, has said (in exaggerated Broadway style), that they do nothing but repeat Broadway successes and formulas. What contribution above mere entertainment—which has its place, to be sure—is made by the well-meaning community theaters around the country when they annually produce warmed-over old Broadway hits?

Rather than imitate Broadway, a major theater should play on Broadway's deficiencies and address its own repertory to its own unique audience. Broadway excels in long-running plays that may involve devastating boredom for the actors. The RAS Theater can offer freedom from boredom and a standard of excellence equal to or surpassing any prospective two- or three-year schedule a performer or his agent might work out in film, television and Broadway!

It is not enough for the RAS Theater to survive, for a survival consciousness might breed timidity. It is not a virtue to survive at the price of relinquishing artistic boldness. Summer stock theaters survive and how many exhibit daring imagination?

Whatever the values and goals of a theater, they should not be static. They should be replaceable by new ones with a constant striving to surpass the last effort. Internal dissent, properly encouraged and handled, will help keep the company's sights high, so long as management is responsive to the "lean and hungry" Cassius-faced members of the theater. The internal dissent must be matched by external dissent. The theater must be willing to schedule plays and events not in agreement with its own policies but which, because they are at variance, stimulate debate, creativity, productivity. Presenting anti-Establishment groups is one way to ensure creative tension.

Management will be presented with many safe roads to take, safe staff to hire, safe companies to bring in, safe ideas to try. *Safety first* may be the chorus song of a conservative board of directors, but it won't be if the board is composed of unsafe and diverse choices. The theater in all aspects must be open to new ideas, new vitality from all directions, the vitality that can lift an audience from its seats with excitement.

The concepts of quality and taste should parallel those of the head of Creative Playthings, a toy manufacturer of quality wooden toys that teach concepts and techniques. No cheap plastic toys or violence-associated playthings, these. The concept is: Give a child toys made of cheap plastics and he'll grow up with a taste for cheap plastic. The theater should heed the late Coco Chanel's famous dictum which ruled her thriving *maison de couture* in Paris: "Let the crowd into the palace and corrupt them with taste."

We need not one but many RAS Theaters in America. I do not believe they will ever evolve from our current regional theaters, and certainly not from Off-Off, Off or Broadway. Each RAS Theater must begin at a running start, fully developed, spectacular and exciting from the first season, under a comprehensive approach to the profession and the community it serves. The reason we cannot expect small theaters to grow into RAS Theaters is that personnel used to thinking in increments of thousands of dollars will take too long to evolve an economy whose increments are in the hundreds of thousands or millions. In the heyday of the Hollywood producer, vanity may have caused some men to think *too* big—but much of what was accomplished would have been impossible otherwise. Many people in the artistic theater tend to think too small, because they have become accustomed to having to fight for every dollar. But inhibition of economic growth due to lack of support or conceptual breadth will only continue to stifle the American theater art.

The RAS Theater should leap into orbit, filled with a spirit of adventure, crewed by a full complement of personnel, equipped with excellent theaters and facilities. Endowed with stability and assertive vigor, the theater would take a commanding role enabling it to present a vast and varied repertory of plays to a community whose lifestyle will be woven into the fabric of the theater.

As a nonprofit cooperative, the RAS Theater is designed to reverse the show business practice that, by benefitting the few, has played havoc with the theater profession. Playwrights, directors and designers have on occasion subsidized the theater with their time, energy and money, but it has been primarily the actor who has sustained American theater through his historic insecurity, the desire to practice his craft having taken precedence over the indignities of the business.

RAS Theaters will provide an institutional core to theater, a home with nurturant growth opportunities that in the musical organizations of America are taken for granted.

A performer's theater is an artistic theater. As a member of a company whose goals are shared, the performer will earn his right to artistic gratification and financial equity. He will be victimized neither by the short-sightedness of typecasting nor the run-of-the-play malaise that contribute so much to Broadway's economy. The performer will be an integral part of a pioneering enterprise that, by serving his own interests, will remove scars too long borne by him.

It will take careful planning, great leadership, imagination, canny judgment, much work and some luck. No one has ever planned or organized a theater along the lines I have been proposing, but it can be done.

Let's take the chance.

Bibliography

Anderson, John. *Box Office*, New York: Jonathan Cape and Harrison Smith, 1929.

Archer, William and Granville-Barker, Henry. *Scheme and Estimates for a National Theater*, New York, Duffield, 1908.

Atkinson, Brooks. *Broadway*, New York: Macmillan, 1970.

Baumol, W. J. and Bowen, W. G. *Performing Arts: The Economic Dilemma*, New York: Twentieth Century Fund, Inc., 1966.

Bentley, Eric. *The Life of the Drama*, New York: Atheneum, 1964.

Blau, Herbert. *The Impossible Theater*, New York: Macmillan, 1964.

Brook, Peter. *The Empty Space*, London: Macgibbon and Key, Ltd., 1968.

Brown, John Russel. *Effective Theatre*, London: Heinemann, 1969.

Brown, Courtney C. and Smith, E. Everett. *The Director Looks at His Job*, New York: Columbia University Press, 1952.

Brustein, Robert. *Revolution as Theatre*, New York: Liveright, 1971.

Brustein, Robert. *Seasons of Discontent*, New York: Simon and Schuster, 1965.

Brustein, Robert. *The Theatre of Revolt*, Boston: Little, Brown & Co., 1964.

Clurman, Harold. *On Directing*, New York: Macmillan, 1972.

Clurman, Harold. *The Fervent Years*, New York, Hill & Wang Dramabook (paperback), 1957.

Friendly, Fred W. *Due to Circumstances Beyond Our Control . . .* , New York: Random House, 1967.

Frohman, Daniel. *Memories of a Manager*, New York: Doubleday, Page & Co., 1911.

Grotowski, Jerzy. *Towards a Poor Theatre*, New York: Simon and Schuster, 1968.

Guthrie, Tyrone. *A New Theatre*, New York: McGraw-Hill, 1964.

Houseman, John. *Run Through*, New York: Simon and Schuster, 1972.

Lilienthal, David E. *Management: A Humanist Art*, New York: Carnegie Institute of Technology, 1967.

Little, Stuart W. and Cantor, Arthur. *The Playmakers*, New York: Norton, 1970.

Morison, Bradley G. and Fliehr, Kay. *In Search of an Audience: How an Audience Was Found for the Tyrone Guthrie Theatre*, New York: Pitman, 1968.

Moskow, Michael H. *Labor Relations in the Performing Arts*, New York: Associated Councils of the Arts, 1969.

Nagler, A. M. *A Source Book in Theatrical History*, New York: Dover, 1952.

Novick, Julius. *Beyond Broadway: The Quest for Permanent Theatres*, New York: Hill & Wang, 1968.

The Performing Arts Problems & Prospects (Rockefeller Panel Report on the future of the theatre, dance, music in America), New York: McGraw-Hill Paperbacks, 1965.

Stagg, Jerry. *The Brothers Shubert*, New York: Random House, 1968.

Taubman, Howard. *The Making of the American Theater*, New York: Coward McCann, 1965.

Tynan, Kenneth. *Curtains*, New York: Atheneum, 1961.

Webster, Margaret. *Don't Put Your Daughter on the Stage*, New York: Alfred A. Knopf, 1972.

Weisman, Philip. *Creativity in Theater: A Psychoanalytic Study*, New York: Delta, 1965.

Index